THE PATH OF PERFECTION

His Divine Grace
A. C. Bhaktivedanta Swami Prabhupāda
Founder-Ācārya of the International Society for Krishna Consciousness

THE BHAKTIVEDANTA BOOK TRUST

Readers interested in the subject matter of this book are invited by the International Society for Krishna Consciousness to visit any ISKCON center worldwide (see address list in back of book) or to correspond with the secretary:

International Society for Krishna Consciousness
P.O. Box 324, Borehamwood, Herts,
WD6 1NB U.K.

International Society for Krishna Consciousness
3764 Watseka Avenue
Los Angeles, California 90034 USA

International Society for Krishna Consciousness
P.O. Box 159, Kings Cross
N.S.W. 2011 Australia

1993 Edition: 120,000 copies

Printed in Germany

ISBN 91-7149-171-6

Contents

Introduction *vii*

1. Yoga as Action 1
2. Mastering the Mind and Senses 14
3. Learning How to See God 28
4. Moderation in Yoga 45
5. Determination and Steadiness in Yoga 70
6. Perception of the Supersoul 86
7. Yoga for the Modern Age 101
8. Failure and Success in Yoga 108
9. Destination After Death 136
10. The Path of Perfection 149

Appendixes

The Author 175

References 179

Glossary 181

Guide to Sanskrit Pronunciation 187

An Introduction to ISKCON and Devotee Life 189

Introduction

When we see a book with a title like *The Path of Perfection,* we may react with a bit of common skepticism: "Oh, another book claiming to give all the answers. One more do-it-yourself enlightenment scheme." And certainly it seems that such skepticism is justified nowadays. Our natural desire for ultimate meaning, happiness, enlightenment, liberation, and salvation has become the most exploited commodity of the twentieth century, creating what one contemporary theologian termed a disastrous "seduction of the spirit". This seduction is, indeed, the most tragic kind of exploitation. And the unfortunate consequence of this exploitation is a kind of deadening cynicism that discourages our search for self-fulfilment and a means to attain it.

The contemporary, thoughtful reader, weary of the many speculative, simplistic books cluttering the bookstore shelves, offering instant formulas for psychological or spiritual salvation, will find *The Path of Perfection* a welcome relief. Herein one will find a clear, intriguing explanation of the philosophy and practice of mankind's oldest system of spiritual development — *yoga.*

Now, the word *yoga* may conjure up an image of some skinny fakir contorted like a human pretzel, or perhaps a room full of corpulent matrons in black leotards struggling to stand on their heads in hope of improving their health, losing weight, or increasing their sexual powers. This is not what we mean by *yoga.* Here we are referring to an ancient philosophy and meditational system that has been practised by millions throughout the ages. What has, in modern times, been reduced to a commercially exploited technique of bodily agility and pseudomeditation was once a comprehensive and easily applied form of self-realisation.

The Path of Perfection consists of a historic series of talks —elaborations on a previously published commentary—by His Divine Grace A.C. Bhaktivedanta Swami Prabhupāda (1896-1977) on India's greatest spiritual classic, the *Bhagavad-gītā.* In these absorbing talks, Śrīla Prabhupāda explores deeply the philosophy of *yoga* as explained in the Sixth and Eighth Chapters of the *Gītā,* showing clearly how these timeless teachings apply to twentieth century mankind. Śrīla Prabhupāda's talks probe questions concerning the nature of consciousness, techniques of meditation, *karma,* death, reincarnation, and even spiritual ecstasy.

The *Bhagavad-gītā,* described by one contemporary psychologist as "a remarkable psychotherapeutic session", appears to us in the form of an extraordinary dialogue between Lord Kṛṣṇa, the Supreme Personality of Godhead, and His warrior disciple Arjuna. Perplexed and confused about his identity and purpose, Arjuna turns to Kṛṣṇa, who reveals "the path of perfection" to His able student. The essence of Lord Kṛṣṇa's teachings is that one must become a *yogī,* that is, one whose life is centred on the practice of *yoga.* And what is *yoga*? The Sanskrit word *yoga* literally means "union", and refers to the union, in love, between the individual consciousness and the Supreme Consciousness, the self and the Superself, the soul and God. *Yoga* is, indeed, "the path of perfection", because it aims toward this most exalted human attainment.

In the *Bhagavad-gītā,* we discover four basic varieties of *yoga* described. *Karma-yoga* refers to the process whereby one performs his work for God, without the selfish desire for personal gain. *Jñāna-yoga* is the process of elevation to spiritual consciousness through the cultivation of philosophical knowledge. The *aṣṭāṅga-yoga* system, of which the modern "*haṭha-yoga*" is a watered-down version, is a mechanical, meditative practice meant to control the mind and senses and focus one's concentration on the Supreme. These three *yoga* systems culminate in *bhakti-yoga*, the *yoga* of selfless, ecstatic, devotional love of God, Kṛṣṇa. Lord Kṛṣṇa Himself states in the last verse of Chapter Six, "Of all *yogīs*, the one with great faith who always abides in Me, thinks of Me within himself, and renders transcendental loving service to Me — he is the most intimately united with Me in *yoga* and is the highest of all."

In *The Path of Perfection*, Śrīla Prabhupāda offers a brilliant summary of the methods of *bhakti-yoga*, revealing the universal applicability of this simple but all-inclusive form of *yoga*. He shows how even those who are entangled in the complexity and chaos of modern materialistic life can begin an uncomplicated practice which purifies the mind and puts one in touch with the Supreme Consciousness.

This, perhaps, was Śrīla Prabhupāda's greatest contribution to our age. Śrīla Prabhupāda was an acknowledged master scholar of India's ancient spiritual culture and of its linguistic foundation, the Sanskrit language. But he was not merely a textual scholar, or a philosopher or theologian engaged in the manufacture of interesting philosophical or theological notions. He was a true spiritual genius who succeeded in bringing to life the essence of India's universal spiritual wisdom in a form which is easy for twentieth century man to understand and practise. This was the unique genius which inspired the late prime minister of India, Sri Lal Bahadur Shastri, to declare openly that the writings of Śrīla Prabhupāda "are a significant contribution to the salvation of mankind." The transforming quality of Śrīla Prabhupāda's writings was also appreciated by sociologist Elwin H. Powell, who commented on Śrīla Prabhupāda's best-selling edition of the *Bhagavad-gītā:* "This transcendental mysticism from the East is now taking root in the 'countercultures' of the West and providing for many a way out of the wilderness of a disintegrating civilisation.... If truth is what works, there must be a kind of truth in the *Bhagavad-gītā As It Is,* since those who follow its teachings display a joyous serenity usually missing in the bleak and strident lives of contemporary people."

— The Publishers

CHAPTER ONE

Yoga as Action

In the Sixth and Eighth Chapters of *Bhagavad-gītā,* Lord Śrī Kṛṣṇa, the Supreme Personality of Godhead, explains that the eightfold *yoga* system is a means to control the mind and senses. This method, however, is very difficult for people to perform, especially in this age of Kali, an age characterised by ignorance and chaos.

Although this eightfold *yoga* system is particularly recommended in the Sixth Chapter of *Bhagavad-gītā,* the Lord emphasises that the process of *karma-yoga,* action in Kṛṣṇa consciousness, is superior. In this world, everyone acts to maintain his family, and everyone is working with a view to some self-interest, or personal sense gratification, be it concentrated or extended. But to act perfectly is to act in Kṛṣṇa consciousness, and this means acting detached from the fruits of labour.

It is our duty to act in Kṛṣṇa consciousness because we are constitutionally parts and parcels of the Supreme. The parts of the body work for the satisfaction of the entire body, not for the individual parts. The goal is the satisfaction of the complete whole. Similarly, the living entity should act for the satisfaction of the supreme whole, the Supreme Personality of Godhead, and not for his own personal satisfaction. One who can do this is the perfect *sannyāsī* and the perfect *yogī.* In the first verse of the Sixth Chapter of *Bhagavad-*

gītā, the chapter dealing with *sāṅkhya-yoga*, Bhagavān Śrī Kṛṣṇa states,

anāśritaḥ karma-phalaṁ
kāryaṁ karma karoti yaḥ
sa sannyāsī ca yogī ca
na niragnir na cākriyaḥ

"One who is unattached to the fruits of his work and who works as he is obligated is in the renounced order of life, and he is the true mystic, not he who lights no fire and performs no duty."

Sometimes *sannyāsīs* (renunciants) incorrectly think that they have become liberated from all material engagements and therefore no longer have to perform *agni-hotra yajñas*, or fire sacrifices. This is a mistake. Certain *yajñas* (sacrifices) have to be performed by everyone for purification. Since *sannyāsīs* are not traditionally required to perform *yajñas*, they sometimes think that they can attain liberation by ceasing to perform the ritualistic *yajñas*, but actually, unless one comes to the platform of Kṛṣṇa consciousness, there is no question of liberation. Those *sannyāsīs* who cease to perform *yajñas* are in fact acting out of self-interest, because their goal is to become one with the impersonal Brahman. That is the ultimate goal of the impersonalists (Māyāvādīs), who have one major goal or demand: to become one with the supreme impersonal Being. The devotees have no such demands. They are simply satisfied in serving Kṛṣṇa for the satisfaction of Kṛṣṇa. They do not want anything in return. That is the characteristic of pure devotion.

It was Lord Caitanya Mahāprabhu who expressed this devotional attitude so succinctly:

na dhanaṁ na janaṁ na sundarīṁ
kavitāṁ vā jagadīśa kāmaye

mama janmani janmanīśvare
bhavatād bhaktir ahaitukī tvayi

"O Almighty Lord, I have no desire to accumulate wealth, nor to enjoy beautiful women. Nor do I want any number of followers. What I want is only the causeless mercy of Your devotional service in my life, birth after birth." (*Śikṣāṣṭaka* 4) In essence, this is the *bhakti-yoga* system. There are many examples of the pure devotional attitude. Once Lord Nṛsiṁhadeva told Prahlāda Mahārāja, "My dear boy, you have suffered so much for Me. Whatever you want, ask for it." Being a pure devotee, Prahlāda Mahārāja refused to ask for anything. He said, "My dear Master, I am not carrying out mercantile business with You. I will not accept any remuneration for my service." This is the pure devotional attitude.

Yogīs and *jñānīs* are demanding to become one with the Supreme because they have such bitter experience suffering the material pangs. They want to become one with the Lord because they are suffering in separation. A pure devotee, however, does not experience this. Although separate from the Lord, he fully enjoys the service of the Lord in separation. The desire to become one with the impersonal Brahman, or to merge with God, is certainly greater than any material desire, but this is not without self-interest. Similarly, the mystic *yogī* who practises the *yoga* system with half-open eyes, ceasing all material activities, desires some satisfaction for his personal self. Such *yogīs* are desirous of material power, and that is their conception of the perfection of *yoga.* Actually, this is not the perfection of *yoga,* but a materialistic process.

If one practises the regulative principles of *yoga,* he can attain eight kinds of perfection. He can become lighter than a cotton swab. He can become heavier than a great stone.

He can immediately get whatever he likes. Sometimes he can even create a planet. Although rare, such powerful *yogīs* actually exist. Viśvāmitra Yogī wanted to beget a man from a palm tree. He was thinking, "Why should a man have to live so many months within the womb of his mother? Why can't he be produced just like a fruit?" Thinking like this, Viśvāmitra Yogī produced men like coconuts. Sometimes *yogīs* are so powerful, they can perform such acts, but these are all material powers. Ultimately such *yogīs* are vanquished, because they cannot retain these material powers indefinitely. *Bhakta-yogīs* are not interested in such powers.

The *bhakti-yogī,* acting in Kṛṣṇa consciousness, works for the satisfaction of the whole without self-interest. A Kṛṣṇa conscious person does not desire self-satisfaction. Rather, his criterion of success is the satisfaction of Kṛṣṇa; therefore he is considered the perfect *sannyāsī* and the perfect *yogī.*

A pure devotee does not even want salvation. The salvationists want to be saved from rebirth, and the voidists also want to put an end to all material life. Caitanya Mahāprabhu, however, requested only devotional service to Lord Kṛṣṇa, birth after birth; in other words, Caitanya Mahāprabhu was prepared to endure material miseries in one body after another. What, then, was Caitanya Mahāprabhu's desire? He wanted to engage in God's service, and nothing more, for that is the real perfection of *yoga.*

Whether in the spiritual sky or the material sky, the individual spirit soul is constitutionally the same. It is said that he is one ten-thousandth part of the tip of a hair. This means that our position is that of a small particle. But spirit can expand. Just as we develop a material body in the material world, we develop a spiritual body in the spiritual world. In the material world, expansion takes place in contact with matter. In the spiritual world, this expansion is spiritual.

Actually, the first lesson of *Bhagavad-gītā* is, "I am spirit soul. I am different from this body." I am a living force, but this material body is not a living force. It is dull matter, and it is activated only because spiritual force is present. In the spiritual world, everything is living force; there is no dead matter. There, the body is totally spiritual. One may compare the spirit soul with oil and the body with water. When oil is in water, there is a distinction, and that distinction always remains. In the spiritual sky, there is no question of oil being placed in water. There everything is spirit.

The impersonalists do not want to develop a body. They simply want to remain spiritual particles, and that is their idea of happiness. But we *bhakti-yogīs* (Vaiṣṇavas) want to serve Kṛṣṇa, and therefore we require hands, legs, and all the other bodily parts. Indeed, we are given these bodies in order to serve Kṛṣṇa. Just as we develop a material body in our mother's womb, we can similarly develop a spiritual body in the spiritual world.

The spiritual body is developed through the practice of Kṛṣṇa consciousness. This material body is spiritualised by this *bhakti-yoga* process. If you place an iron within fire, the iron becomes so hot that it also becomes fiery. When the iron is red hot, it acquires all the qualities of fire. If you touch something with that iron, that iron will act as fire. Similarly, although this body is material, it can become spiritualised through Kṛṣṇa consciousness and act as spirit. Although copper is just a metal, as soon as it comes in contact with electricity, it becomes electrified, and if you touch it, you will receive an electric shock.

As soon as your body is spiritualised, material activity ceases. Material activity means acting for sense gratification. As you become spiritualised, material demands dwindle until they become nil. How is this possible? In order for an iron to act as fire, it must remain constantly in contact with fire. In order for the material body to become spiritualised, one must remain constantly in Kṛṣṇa consciousness. When this material body is fully engaged in spiritual activities, it becomes spiritual.

According to the Vedic system, the body of a high personality, a *sannyāsī,* is not burned but buried, because a *sannyāsī's* body is considered spiritual, having ceased to engage in material activities. If everyone in this world engages fully in Kṛṣṇa consciousness and ceases to work for sense gratification, this entire world will immediately become spiritual. Therefore it is necessary to learn how to work for the satisfaction of Kṛṣṇa. This requires a little time to understand. If something is used for Kṛṣṇa's satisfaction, it is spiritual. Since we are using microphones, typewriters, etc., in order to talk and write about Kṛṣṇa, they become spiritualised. What is the difference between *prasādam* and ordinary food? Some people may say, "What is this *prasādam*? We are eating the same food. Why do you call it *prasādam*?" It is *prasādam* because it has been offered for Kṛṣṇa's satisfaction and has thus become spiritualised.

In a higher sense, there is no matter at all. Everything is spiritual. Because Kṛṣṇa is spiritual and matter is one of the energies of Kṛṣṇa, matter is also spiritual. Kṛṣṇa is totally spiritual, and spirit comes from spirit. However, because the living entities are misusing this energy — that is, using it for something other than Kṛṣṇa's purposes — it becomes materialised, and so we call it matter. The purpose of this Kṛṣṇa consciousness movement is to *respiritualise* this energy. It is our purpose to respiritualise the whole world, socially and politically. Of course, this may not be possible, but it is our ideal. At least if we individually take up this respiritualisation process, our lives become perfect.

In *Bhagavad-gītā* (9.22) Kṛṣṇa says that He provides for His devotees by giving them what they lack and preserving what they have. People are very fond of saying that God helps those who help themselves, but they do not understand that helping yourself means putting yourself under Kṛṣṇa's protection. If one thinks, "Oh, I can help myself. I can protect myself," one is thinking foolishly. As long as my finger is attached to my body, it is useful, and I may spend thousands of pounds to preserve it. But if this finger is cut off, it is useless and is thrown away. Similarly, we are part and parcel of Kṛṣṇa, and helping ourselves means putting ourselves in our proper position as His parts and parcels. Otherwise we are only fit to be cast away. The finger can help itself only when situated properly on the hand and working on behalf of the entire body. If the finger thinks, "I will separate myself from this body and simply help myself," that finger will be cast away and will die. As soon as we think, "I shall live independently of Kṛṣṇa," that is our spiritual death, and as soon as we engage in Kṛṣṇa's service, as His part and parcel, that is our spiritual life. Therefore, helping oneself means knowing one's actual position and working accordingly. It is not possible to help oneself without knowing one's position.

Service means activity, for when we serve someone, we are acting. When we serve Kṛṣṇa, we are preaching Kṛṣṇa consciousness, or cooking, or cleansing the temple, or distributing books about Kṛṣṇa, or writing about Him or shopping for foodstuff to offer Him. There are so many ways to serve. Helping Kṛṣṇa means acting for Him, not sitting down in one place and artificially meditating. Kṛṣṇa consciousness means activity. Whatever assets we have should be utilised for Kṛṣṇa. That is the process of *bhakti-yoga*. Kṛṣṇa has given us a mind, and we must utilise this mind to think of

Kṛṣṇa. We have been given these hands, and we must use them to wash the temple or cook for Kṛṣṇa. We have been given these legs, and we should use them to go to the temple of Kṛṣṇa. We have been given a nose, and we should use it to smell the flowers that have been offered to Kṛṣṇa. Through the process of *bhakti-yoga,* we engage all these senses in the service of Kṛṣṇa, and in this way the senses are spiritualised.

In *Bhagavad-gītā,* Arjuna was refusing to act, and Kṛṣṇa was inspiring him to engage in activity. The entire *Bhagavad-gītā* is an inspiration to work, to engage in Kṛṣṇa consciousness, to act on Kṛṣṇa's behalf. Kṛṣṇa never tells Arjuna, "My dear friend Arjuna, don't concern yourself with this war. Just sit down and meditate upon Me." This is not the message of *Bhagavad-gītā.* We are not to refrain from all activity, but only from those activities that impede our consciousness of Kṛṣṇa. Meditation means stopping all nonsensical activity. Those who are advanced in Kṛṣṇa consciousness are constantly working for Kṛṣṇa.

A mother tells only her bad child to sit down and do nothing. If a child can do nothing but disturb his mother, the mother says, "My dear child, just sit down here and keep quiet." But if the child can work nicely, the mother says, "My dear child, will you please help me do this? Will you go over there and do that?" Sitting still in one place is just for those who do not know how to work sensibly. As long as the child sits in one place, he does not raise havoc. Sitting still means negating nonsense; it is not positive activity. In negation, there is no life. Positive activities constitute life, and positive activity is the message of *Bhagavad-gītā.* Spiritual life is not "Don't do this." Spiritual life is "*Do this*!" In order to act properly, there are certain things that one must know not to do; therefore certain activities are forbidden. The whole *Bhagavad-gītā,* however, is "*do*". Kṛṣṇa says,

"Fight for Me." At the beginning of *Bhagavad-gītā*, when Arjuna told Kṛṣṇa, "I will not fight," Śrī Kṛṣṇa said,

kutas tvā kaśmalam idaṁ
viṣame samupasthitam
anārya-juṣṭam asvargyam
akīrti-karam arjuna

"My dear Arjuna, how have these impurities come upon you? They are not at all befitting a man who knows the value of life. They lead not to higher planets but to infamy." (Bg. 2.2) Kṛṣṇa directly tells Arjuna that he is speaking like a non-Āryan — that is, like one who does not know the spiritual values of life. So Kṛṣṇa consciousness does not mean sitting down idly.

Kṛṣṇa Himself does not sit down idly. All His pastimes are filled with activity. When we go to the spiritual world, we will see that Kṛṣṇa is always engaged in dancing, eating, and enjoying. He does not sit down to meditate. Is there any account of the *gopīs* meditating? Did Caitanya Mahāprabhu sit down to meditate? No, He was always dancing and chanting Hare Kṛṣṇa. The spirit soul is naturally active. How can we sit down silently and do nothing? It is not possible. Therefore, after Śrī Kṛṣṇa outlined the *sāṅkhya-yoga* system in the Sixth Chapter of *Bhagavad-gītā*, Arjuna frankly said,

yo 'yaṁ yogas tvayā proktaḥ
sāmyena madhusūdana
etasyāhaṁ na paśyāmi
cañcalatvāt sthitiṁ sthirām

"O Madhusūdana [Kṛṣṇa], the system of *yoga* which You have summarised appears impractical and unendurable to me, for the mind is restless and unsteady." (Bg. 6.33) Although Arjuna was highly elevated and was Kṛṣṇa's intimate friend, he immediately refused to take up this *sāṅkhya-yoga* system. In essence, he said, "It is not possible for me." How could it have been possible? Arjuna was a warrior, a householder, and he wanted a kingdom. What time did he have for meditation? He flatly refused to practise this type of meditational *yoga*, saying that the mind is as difficult to control as the wind (Bg. 6.34). That is a fact. It is not possible to control the mind artificially; therefore we must engage the mind in Kṛṣṇa consciousness. Then it is controlled. If Arjuna found this process more difficult than controlling the wind, then what of us? After all, Arjuna was not an ordinary man. He was personally talking with the Supreme Lord, Śrī Kṛṣṇa, and he proclaimed the mind to be like a great wind. How can we control the wind? We can control the mind only by fixing it on Kṛṣṇa's lotus feet. That is the perfection of meditation.

No one really wants to sit down and meditate. Why should we? We're meant for positive activity, for recreation, for pleasure. In Kṛṣṇa consciousness, our recreation is dancing and chanting, and when we get tired, we take *prasādam*. Is dancing difficult? Is chanting difficult? We don't charge anything to dance in the temple. If you go to a ballroom, you have to pay to enter, but we do not charge. It is natural to enjoy music and dancing and palatable foods. These are our recreations, and this is our method of meditation. So this *yoga* system is not at all laborious. It is simply recreation, *susukham*. It is stated in the Ninth Chapter of *Bhagavad-gītā* (9.2) that this *yoga* is *susukham* — very happy. "It is everlasting, and it is joyfully performed." It is natural, automatic, and spontaneous. It is our real life in the spiritual world.

In Vaikuṇṭha, the spiritual world, there is no anxiety. *Vaikuṇṭha* means "freedom from anxiety", and in Vaikuṇṭha the liberated souls are always dancing, chanting and taking *prasādam.* There are no factories, hard work, or technical institutions. There is no need for these artificial things. In *Vedānta-sūtra* it is stated, *ānanda-mayo 'bhyāsāt:* God is *ānanda-maya,* full of bliss and pleasure. Since we are part and parcel of God, we also possess these same qualities. So the goal of our *yoga* process is to join with the supreme *ānanda-maya,* Śrī Kṛṣṇa, to join His dance party. Then we will be actually happy.

On this earth we are trying to be happy artificially and are therefore frustrated. Once we are situated in Kṛṣṇa consciousness, we will revive our original position and become simply joyful. Since our actual nature is *ānanda-maya,* blissful, we are always searching for happiness. In the cities we are inundated with advertisements. Restaurants, bars, nightclubs and dance halls are always announcing, "Come on, here is *ānanda.* Here is pleasure." That is because everyone is searching for *ānanda,* pleasure. Our society for Kṛṣṇa consciousness is also announcing, "Here is *ānanda,*" but our standard of pleasure is very different. In any case, the goal — pleasure — is the same.

Most people are hunting for pleasure on the gross material platform. The more advanced search for pleasure in speculation, philosophy, poetry or art. The *bhakti-yogī,* however, searches for pleasure on the transcendental platform, and that is his only business. Why are people working so hard all day? They are thinking, "Tonight I shall enjoy. Tonight I will associate with this girl or with my wife." Thus people are going to so much trouble to acquire a little pleasure. Pleasure is the ultimate goal, but unfortunately, under illusion, people do not know where real pleasure is to be found. Real pleasure exists eternally in the transcendental form of Kṛṣṇa.

Perhaps you have seen pictures of Kṛṣṇa, and if so, you

have noticed that Kṛṣṇa is always jolly. If you join His society, you will also become jolly. Have you ever seen pictures of Kṛṣṇa working with a machine? Have you ever seen pictures of Kṛṣṇa smoking? No, He is *by nature* full of pleasure, and if you unfold yourself in that way, you will also find pleasure. Pleasure cannot be found artificially.

ānanda-cinmaya-rasa-pratibhāvitābhis
tābhir ya eva nija-rūpatayā kalābhiḥ
goloka eva nivasaty akhilātma-bhūto
govindam ādi-puruṣaṁ tam ahaṁ bhajāmi

"I worship Govinda, the primeval Lord, residing in His own realm, Goloka, with Rādhā, resembling His own spiritual figure, the embodiment of the ecstatic potency possessed of the sixty-four artistic activities, in the company of Her confidantes (*sakhīs*), embodiments of the extensions of Her bodily form, permeated and vitalised by His ever-blissful spiritual *rasa*." (*Brahma-saṁhitā* 5.37)

The word *rasa* means "taste", or "mellow". We enjoy sweets or candy because of their taste. Everyone is trying to enjoy some taste, and we want to enjoy sex because there is some taste there. That is called *ādi* taste. Material tastes are different because they are tasted and quickly finished. Material tastes last only a few minutes. You may take a piece of candy, taste it, and say, "Oh, that is very nice," but you have to taste another in order to continue the enjoyment. Material taste is not unlimited, but real taste is without end. Spiritual taste cannot be forgotten; it goes on increasing. *Ānandāmbudhi-vardhanam.* Caitanya Mahāprabhu says, "This taste is always increasing." Spiritual taste is like the ocean in the sense that it is very great. The Pacific Ocean is always tossing, but it is not increasing. By God's order, the ocean does not extend beyond its limit, and if it extends, there is havoc.

Lord Caitanya Mahāprabhu says that there is another ocean, an ocean of transcendental bliss, an ocean that is always increasing. *Ānandāmbudhi-vardhanaṁ pratipadaṁ pūrṇāmṛtāsvādanaṁ/ sarvātma-snapanaṁ paraṁ vijayate śrī-kṛṣṇa-saṅkīrtanam.* By chanting Hare Kṛṣṇa, our pleasure potency increases more and more.

One who has realised Śrī Kṛṣṇa is always living in Vṛndāvana, Vaikuṇṭha. Although a devotee may seem to be living in some place far from Vṛndāvana, he is always living in Vṛndāvana, because he knows that Kṛṣṇa is present everywhere, even within the atom. The Supreme Lord is bigger than the biggest and smaller than the smallest. Once we are fully realised and established in Kṛṣṇa consciousness, we never lose sight of Kṛṣṇa, and our bliss is always increasing. This is the true *yoga* system, *bhakti-yoga*, as expounded by Lord Śrī Kṛṣṇa Himself in *Bhagavad-gītā*.

CHAPTER TWO

Mastering the Mind and Senses

yaṁ sannyāsam iti prāhur
yogaṁ taṁ viddhi pāṇḍava
na hy asannyasta-saṅkalpo
yogī bhavati kaścana

"What is called renunciation you should know to be the same as *yoga,* or linking oneself with the Supreme, for one can never become a *yogī* unless he renounces the desire for sense gratification." (Bg. 6.2)

This is the real purpose of the practice of *yoga.* The word *yoga* means "to join". Although we are naturally part and parcel of the Supreme, in our conditioned state we are now separated. Because of our separation, we are reluctant to understand God and to speak of our relationship with Him and are even inclined to think of such discussion as a waste of time. In a church or in a Kṛṣṇa consciousness temple, we speak of God, but people in general are not very interested. They think it is a waste of time, a kind of recreation in the name of spiritual advancement, and they believe that this time could be better used to earn money or enjoy themselves in a nightclub or restaurant.

Therefore, it is due to sense enjoyment that we are not attracted to God, and therefore it is said that those who are addicted to sense enjoyment cannot become *yogīs* — that is, they are not eligible to participate in the *yoga* system. One cannot advance in any *yoga* system if he partakes in sense gratification and then sits down to try to meditate. This is just a colossal hoax. Such contradictory activity has no meaning. First of all, *yoga* means controlling the senses — *yama-niyama.* There are eight stages of *yoga* — *yama, niyama, āsana, dhyāna, dhāraṇā, prāṇāyāma, pratyāhāra,* and *samādhi.*

In this Sixth Chapter, in which the Lord speaks of the *sāṅkhya-yoga* system, He states from the very beginning that one cannot become a *yogī* unless one renounces the desire for sense gratification. Therefore, if one indulges his senses, he cannot be accepted as a *yogī. Yoga* demands strict celibacy. In the *yoga* system, there is no sex life. If one indulges in sex, he cannot be a *yogī.* Many so-called *yogīs* come from India to England and say, "Yes, you can do whatever you like. You can have as much sex as you like. Just meditate. I will give you some *mantra,* and you will give me some money." This is all nonsense. According to the authoritative statements of Śrī Kṛṣṇa, one cannot become a *yogī* unless he renounces the desire for sense gratification. This is explicitly stated as the first condition for *yoga* practice.

ārurukṣor muner yogaṁ
karma kāraṇam ucyate
yogārūḍhasya tasyaiva
śamaḥ kāraṇam ucyate

"For one who is a neophyte in the eightfold *yoga* system, work is said to be the means; and for one who is already elevated in *yoga,* cessation of all material activities is said to be the means." (Bg. 6.3) According to this verse, there are those who are attempting to reach the perfectional stage and those who have already attained that stage. As long as one is not situated on the perfectional platform, he must engage in so many works. In the West, there are many *yoga* societies attempting to practise the *āsana* system, and therefore they practise sitting in different postures. That may help, but it is only a process by which one can attain the real platform. The real *yoga* system, in its perfectional stage, is far different from these bodily gymnastics.

It is important to understand, however, that from the beginning, a Kṛṣṇa conscious person is situated on the platform of meditation because he is always thinking of Kṛṣṇa. Being constantly engaged in the service of Kṛṣṇa, he is considered to have ceased all material activities.

yadā hi nendriyārtheṣu
na karmasv anuṣajjate
sarva-saṅkalpa-sannyāsī
yogārūḍhas tadocyate

"A person is said to be elevated in *yoga* when, having renounced all material desires, he neither acts for sense gratification nor engages in fruitive activities." (Bg. 6.4)

This is actually the perfectional stage of *yoga,* and one who has attained this stage is said to have attained to *yoga.* This is to say that he has connected, joined, or linked himself with the supreme whole. If a part is disconnected from a machine, it serves no function, but as soon as it is properly attached to the machine, it works properly and carries out its different functions. That is the meaning of *yoga* — joining with the supreme whole, serving in conjunction with the total machine. Presently we are disconnected, and our material fruitive activities are simply a waste of time. One who engages in such activity is described in *Bhagavad-gītā* as a *mūḍha* — that is, a rascal. Although one may earn thousands of pounds daily and be an important businessman, he is described in *Bhagavad-gītā* as a *mūḍha,* rascal, because he is just wasting his time in eating, sleeping, defending, and mating.

People do not stop to consider that they are actually working very hard for nothing. One who earns millions of pounds cannot really eat much more than a man who makes ten pounds. A man who earns millions of pounds cannot mate with millions of women. That is not within his power. His mating power is the same as one who earns ten pounds, just as his power of eating is the same. This is to say that our power of enjoyment is limited. One should therefore think, "My enjoyment is the same as that of the man who is earning ten pounds daily. So why am I working so hard to earn millions of pounds? Why am I wasting my energy? I should engage my time and energy in understanding God. That is the purpose of life." If one has no economic problems, he has sufficient time to understand Kṛṣṇa consciousness. If he wastes this precious time, he is called a *mūḍha,* a rascal or an ass.

According to the preceding verse, a person is said to have attained *yoga* when he has renounced all material desires. Once we are situated perfectly in *yoga,* we are satisfied. We no longer experience material desires. We no longer act for sense gratification or engage in fruitive activity. When we speak of "fruitive activity", we refer to activities carried out for the purpose of sense gratification. That is, we are earning money in order to gratify our senses. If one is virtuous, he engages in pious activities — he donates money to charities, opens hospitals, schools, etc. Although these are certainly virtuous activities, they are ultimately meant for sense gratification. How is this? If I donate to an educational institution, for instance, I will receive good educational facilities and will become highly educated in my next life. Being thus educated, I will attain a good position and will acquire a good amount of money. Then how will I utilise this money? For sense gratification. Thus these virtuous and fruitive activities form a kind of cycle.

We often hear the expression "a better standard of life", but what does this mean? It is said that the standard of life in England is superior to that in India, but in both countries there is eating, sleeping, defending, and mating. Of course, in England the quality of food may be better, but the eating process is there. A superior standard of life does not mean superior spiritual realisation. It just means better eating, sleeping, mating and defending. This is called fruitive activity, and it is based on sense gratification.

Yoga has nothing to do with sense gratification or fruitive activity. *Yoga* means connecting with the Supreme. Dhruva Mahārāja underwent severe austerities in order to see God, and when he finally saw God, he said, *svāmin kṛtārtho 'smi varaṁ na yāce:* "My dear Lord, I am now fully satisfied. I am not asking for anything more. I do not want any further benediction from You." Why didn't Dhruva Mahārāja ask for benedictions? What is a "benediction"? Generally, *benediction* means receiving a great kingdom, a beautiful wife, palatable food, and so forth, but when one is actually connected with God, he does not want such "benedictions". He is fully satisfied. *Svāmin kṛtārtho 'smi varaṁ na yāce.*

Actually, Dhruva Mahārāja initially searched for God in order to attain his father's kingdom. Dhruva Mahārāja's mother was rejected by his father, and his stepmother resented his sitting on his father's lap. Indeed, she forbade him to sit on his father's lap because Dhruva Mahārāja was not born in her womb. Although only five years old, Dhruva Mahārāja was a *kṣatriya,* and he took this as a great insult. Going to his own mother, he said, "Mother, my stepmother has insulted me by forbidding me to sit on my father's lap." Dhruva Mahārāja then started to cry, and his mother said, "My dear boy, what can I do? Your father loves your stepmother more than he loves me. I can do nothing." Dhruva

Mahārāja then said, "But I want my father's kingdom. Tell me how I can get it." "My dear boy," his mother said, "if Kṛṣṇa, God, blesses you, you can get it." "Where is God?" Dhruva Mahārāja asked. "Oh, it is said that God is in the forest," his mother said. "Great sages go to the forest to search for God."

Hearing this, Dhruva Mahārāja went directly to the forest and began to perform severe penances. Finally he saw God, and when he saw Him, he no longer desired his father's kingdom. Instead, he said, "My dear Lord, I was searching for some pebbles, but instead I have found valuable jewels. I no longer care for my father's kingdom. Now I am fully satisfied." When one is actually connected with God, he is totally satisfied. His satisfaction is infinitely greater than so-called enjoyment in this material world. That is the satisfaction resulting from God realisation, and that is the perfection of *yoga.*

When a person is fully engaged in the transcendental loving service of the Lord, he is pleased in himself, and thus he is no longer engaged in sense gratification or in fruitive activities. Otherwise, one must be engaged in sense gratification, since one cannot live without engagement. It is impossible to cease all activity. As stated before, it is our nature as living entities to act. It is said, "An idle mind is the devil's workshop." If we have no Kṛṣṇa conscious engagement, we will engage in sense gratification or fruitive activity. If a child is not trained or educated, he becomes spoiled. If one does not practise the *yoga* system, if he does not attempt to control his senses by the *yoga* process, he will engage his senses in their own gratification. When one is gratifying his senses, there is no question of practising *yoga.*

Without Kṛṣṇa consciousness, one must be always seeking self-centred or extended selfish activities. But a Kṛṣṇa conscious person can do everything for the satisfaction of Kṛṣṇa and thereby be perfectly detached from sense gratification. One who has not realised Kṛṣṇa must mechanically try to escape material desires before being elevated to the top rung of the *yoga* ladder.

One may compare the *yoga* system to a stepladder. One *yogī* may be situated on the fifth step, another *yogī* may be on the fiftieth step and yet another on the five-hundredth step. The purpose, of course, is to reach the top. Although the entire ladder may be called the *yoga* system, one who is on the fifth step is not equal to one who is higher up. In *Bhagavad-gītā*, Śrī Kṛṣṇa delineates a number of *yoga* systems — *karma-yoga, jñāna-yoga, dhyāna-yoga,* and *bhakti-yoga*. All of these systems are connected with God, Kṛṣṇa, just as the entire ladder is connected to the topmost floor. This is not to say that everyone practising the *yoga* system is situated on the topmost floor; only he who is in full Kṛṣṇa consciousness is so situated. Others are situated on different steps of the yogic ladder.

uddhared ātmanātmānaṁ
nātmānam avasādayet
ātmaiva hy ātmano bandhur
ātmaiva ripur ātmanaḥ

"One must deliver himself with the help of his mind, and not degrade himself. The mind is the friend of the conditioned soul, and his enemy as well." (Bg. 6.5) The word *ātmā* denotes body, mind, and soul — depending on different circumstances. In the *yoga* system, the mind and the conditioned soul are especially important. Since the mind is the central point of *yoga* practice, *ātmā* refers here to the mind. The purpose of the *yoga* system is to control the mind and to draw it away from attachment to sense objects. It is stressed herein that the mind must be so trained that it can deliver the conditioned soul from the mire of nescience.

In the *aṣṭāṅga-yoga* system, these eightfold *yogas* — *dhyāna, dhāraṇā,* etc. — are meant to control the mind. Śrī Kṛṣṇa explicitly states that a man must utilise his mind to elevate himself. Unless one can control the mind, there is no question of elevation. The body is like a chariot, and the mind is the driver. If you tell your driver, "Please take me to the Kṛṣṇa temple," the driver will take you there, but if you tell him, "Please take me to that liquor house," you will go there. It is the driver's business to take you wherever you like. If you can control the driver, he will take you where you should go, but if not, he will ultimately take you wherever he likes. If you have no control over your driver, your driver is your enemy, but if he acts according to your orders, he is your friend.

The *yoga* system is meant to control the mind in such a way that the mind will act as your friend. Sometimes the mind acts as a friend and sometimes as an enemy. Because we are part and parcel of the Supreme, who has infinite independence, we have minute, or finite, independence. It is the mind that is controlling that independence, and therefore he may either take us to the Kṛṣṇa temple or to some nightclub.

It is the purpose of this Kṛṣṇa consciousness movement to fix the mind on Kṛṣṇa. When the mind is so fixed, he cannot do anything but act as our friend. He has no scope to act any other way. As soon as Kṛṣṇa is seated in the mind, there is light, just as when the sun is in the sky, darkness is vanquished. Kṛṣṇa is just like the sun, and when He is present, there is no scope for darkness. If we keep Kṛṣṇa on our mind, the darkness of *māyā* will never be able to enter.

Keeping the mind fixed on Kṛṣṇa is the perfection of *yoga.* If the mind is strongly fixed on the Supreme, it will not allow any nonsense to enter, and there will be no falldown. If the mind is strong, the driver is strong, and we may go wherever we may desire. The entire *yoga* system is meant to make the mind strong, to make it incapable of deviating from the Supreme.

Sa vai manaḥ kṛṣṇa-padāravindayoḥ. One should fix his mind on Kṛṣṇa, just as Ambarīṣa Mahārāja did when he had a fight with a great *aṣṭāṅga-yogī* named Durvāsā Muni. Since Ambarīṣa Mahārāja was a householder, he was a pounds-shillings man. This means that he had to take into account pounds, shillings, and sixpence. Apart from being a householder, Mahārāja Ambarīṣa was also a great king and devotee. Durvāsā Muni was a great *yogī* who happened to be very envious of Mahārāja Ambarīṣa. Durvāsā Muni was thinking, "I am a great *yogī,* and I can travel in space. This man is an ordinary king, and he does not possess such yogic powers. Still, people pay him more honour. Why is this? I will teach him a good lesson." Durvāsā Muni then proceeded to pick a quarrel with Mahārāja Ambarīṣa, but because the king was always thinking of Kṛṣṇa, he managed to defeat this great *yogī.* Durvāsā Muni was consequently directed by Nārāyaṇa to take shelter at the feet of Mahārāja Ambarīṣa. Durvāsā Muni was such a perfect *yogī* that within a year he could travel throughout the material universe and also penetrate the spiritual universe. Indeed, he went directly to the abode of God, Vaikuṇṭha, and saw the Personality of Godhead Himself. Yet Durvāsā Muni was so weak that he had to return to earth and fall at the feet of Mahārāja Ambarīṣa. Mahārāja Ambarīṣa was an ordinary king, but his one great qualification was that he was always thinking of Kṛṣṇa. Thus his mind was always controlled, and he was situated at the highest perfectional level of *yoga.* We also can very easily control the mind by keeping it fixed on the lotus feet of Kṛṣṇa within. Simply by thinking of Kṛṣṇa, we become victorious conquerors, topmost *yogīs.*

Yoga indriya-saṁyamaḥ. The *yoga* system is meant to control the senses, and since the mind is above the senses, if we can control the mind, our senses are automatically controlled. The tongue may want to eat something improper, but if the mind is strong, it can say, "No. You cannot eat this. You can only eat *kṛṣṇa-prasāda.*" In this way the tongue, as well as all the other senses, can be controlled by the mind. *Indriyāṇi parāṇy āhur indriyebhyaḥ paraṁ manaḥ.* The material body consists of the senses, and consequently the body's activities are sensual activities. However, above the senses is the mind, and above the mind is the intelligence, and above the intelligence is the spirit soul. If one is on the spiritual platform, his intelligence, mind, and senses are all spiritualised. The purpose of this Kṛṣṇa consciousness process is to actualise the spiritualisation of senses, mind, and intelligence. The spirit soul is superior to all, but because he is sleeping, he has given power of attorney to the fickle mind. However, when the soul is awakened, he is once again master, and the servile mind cannot act improperly. Once we are awakened in Kṛṣṇa consciousness, the intelligence, mind, and senses cannot act nonsensically. They must act in accordance with the dictations of the spirit soul. That is spiritualisation and purification. *Hṛṣīkeṇa hṛṣīkeśa-sevanaṁ bhaktir ucyate.* We must serve the master of the senses with the senses. The Supreme Lord is called Hṛṣīkeśa, which means that He is the original controller of the senses, just as a king is the original controller of all the activities of a state, and the citizens are secondary controllers.

Bhakti means acting spiritually in accordance with the desires of Hṛṣīkeśa. How can we act? Since we must act with our senses, we must spiritualise our senses in order to act properly. As stated before, sitting in silent meditation means stopping undesirable activity, but acting in Kṛṣṇa consciousness is transcendental. The cessation of nonsensical action is not in itself perfection. We must *act* perfectly. Unless we train our senses to act in accordance with Hṛṣīkeśa, the master of the senses, our senses will again engage in undesirable activities, and we will fall down. Therefore we must engage the senses in action for Kṛṣṇa and in this way remain firmly fixed in Kṛṣṇa consciousness.

In material existence one is subjected to the influence of the mind and the senses. In fact, the pure soul is entangled in the material world because of the mind's ego, which desires to lord it over material nature. Therefore the mind should be trained so that it will not be attracted by the glitter of material nature, and in this way the conditioned soul may be saved. One should not degrade oneself by attraction to sense objects. The more one is attracted by sense objects, the more one becomes entangled in material existence. The best way to disentangle oneself is to always engage the mind in Kṛṣṇa consciousness. The word *hi* in verse 5, Chapter Six (*Bhagavad-gītā*), is used to emphasise this point — namely, that one *must* do this. It is also said,

mana eva manuṣyāṇāṁ
kāraṇaṁ bandha-mokṣayoḥ
bandhāya viṣayāsaṅgi
muktyai nirviṣayaṁ manaḥ

"For man, mind is the cause of bondage and mind is the cause of liberation. Mind absorbed in sense objects is the cause of bondage, and mind detached from the sense objects is the cause of liberation." (*Viṣṇu Purāṇa* 6.7.28) The mind which is always engaged in Kṛṣṇa consciousness is the cause of supreme liberation. When the mind is thus engaged in Kṛṣṇa consciousness, there is no chance of its being engaged in *māyā* consciousness. In Kṛṣṇa consciousness, we remain in the sunlight, and there is no chance of our being obscured by darkness.

Because we have freedom, or liberty, we can stay within a dark room or go out into the broad daylight. That is our choice. Darkness can be eradicated by light, but light cannot be covered by darkness. If we are in a dark room and someone brings in a lamp, the darkness is vanquished. But we cannot take darkness into the sunlight. It is not possible. The darkness will simply fade away. *Kṛṣṇa sūrya-sama māyā haya andhakāra.* Kṛṣṇa is like sunlight, and *māyā* is like darkness. So how can darkness exist in sunlight? If we always keep ourselves in the sunlight, darkness will fail to act upon us. This is the whole philosophy of Kṛṣṇa consciousness: always engage in Kṛṣṇa conscious activities, and *māyā* will be dissipated, just as darkness is dissipated when there is light. This is stated in *Śrīmad-Bhāgavatam* (1.7.4):

bhakti-yogena manasi
samyak praṇihite 'male
apaśyat puruṣaṁ pūrṇaṁ
māyāṁ ca tad-apāśrayam

"When the sage Vyāsadeva, under the instruction of his spiritual master, Nārada, fixed his mind, perfectly engaging it by linking it in devotional service (*bhakti-yoga*) without any tinge of materialism, Vyāsadeva saw the Absolute Personality of Godhead, along with His external energy, which was under full control."

The word *manasi* refers to the mind. When one is enlightened in *bhakti-yoga*, the mind becomes completely freed from all contamination (*samyak praṇihite 'male*). When Vyāsa saw the Supreme Personality of Godhead, he saw *māyā* in the background (*māyāṁ ca tad-apāśrayam*). Whenever there is light, there is also the possibility of darkness being present. That is, darkness is the other side of light, or darkness is under the shelter of light, just as if I hold my hand up to the light, the top part of my hand will be in light, and the bottom part will be shaded. In other words, one side is light and the other darkness. When Vyāsadeva saw Kṛṣṇa, the Supreme Lord, he also saw *māyā*, darkness, under His shelter.

And what is this *māyā*? This is explained in the next verse of *Śrīmad-Bhāgavatam* (1.7.5):

yayā sammohito jīva
ātmānaṁ tri-guṇātmakam
paro 'pi manute 'narthaṁ
tat-kṛtaṁ cābhipadyate

"Due to the external energy, the living entity, although transcendental to the three modes of material nature, thinks of himself as a material product and thus undergoes the reactions of material miseries." Thus the illusory energy has temporarily covered the conditioned souls. And who are these conditioned souls? Although finite, the conditioned spirit souls are as full of light as Kṛṣṇa. The problem is that the conditioned soul identifies himself with this material world. This is called illusion, false identification with matter. Although the individual spirit soul is transcendental, he engages in improper activities under the dictation of *māyā*, and this brings about his conditioning or false identification. This is very elaborately explained in the Seventh Chapter, First Canto, of *Śrīmad-Bhāgavatam*.

In conclusion, our actual position is that of spiritual sparks, full of light. Now we are temporarily covered by this illusory energy, *māyā*, which is dictating to us. Acting under the influence of *māyā*, we are becoming more and more entangled in the material energy. The *yoga* system is meant to disentangle us, and the perfection of *yoga* is Kṛṣṇa consciousness. Thus Kṛṣṇa consciousness is the most effective means by which we can disentangle ourselves from the influence of the material energy.

CHAPTER THREE

Learning How to See God

bandhur ātmātmanas tasya
yenātmaivātmanā jitaḥ
anātmanas tu śatrutve
vartetātmaiva śatru-vat

"For him who has conquered the mind, the mind is the best of friends; but for one who has failed to do so, his mind will remain the greatest enemy." (Bg. 6.6)

The purpose of the *yoga* system is to make the mind into a friend instead of an enemy. In material contact, the mind is in a kind of drunken condition. As stated in *Caitanya-caritāmṛta* (*Madhya-līlā* 20.117),

kṛṣṇa bhuli' sei jīva—anādi-bahirmukha
ataeva māyā tāre deya saṁsāra-duḥkha

"Forgetting Kṛṣṇa, the living entity has been attracted by the Lord's external feature from time immemorial. Therefore the illusory energy (*māyā*) gives him all kinds of misery in his material existence." The living entity is constitutionally spirit soul, part and parcel of the Supreme Lord. As soon as the mind is contaminated, the living entity, because he has a little independence, rebels. In this state, the mind dictates, "Why should I serve Kṛṣṇa? I am God." Thus one labours under a false impression, and his life is spoiled. We try to conquer many things — even empires — but if we fail to conquer the mind, we are failures even if we manage to conquer an empire. Even though emperors, we will have within us our greatest enemy — our own mind.

jitātmanaḥ praśāntasya
paramātmā samāhitaḥ
śītoṣṇa-sukha-duḥkheṣu
tathā mānāpamānayoḥ

"For one who has conquered the mind, the Supersoul is already reached, for he has attained tranquillity. To such a man happiness and distress, heat and cold, honour and dishonour are all the same." (Bg. 6.7)

Actually, every living entity is intended to abide by the dictation of the Supreme Personality of Godhead, who is seated in everyone's heart as Paramātmā. When the mind is misled by the external illusory energy, one becomes entangled in material activities. Therefore, as soon as one's mind is controlled through one of the *yoga* systems, one is to be considered as having already reached the destination. One has to abide by superior dictation. When the mind is fixed on the superior nature, he has no alternative but to follow the dictation of the Supreme. The mind must admit some superior dictation and follow it. When the mind is controlled, one automatically follows the dictation of the Paramātmā, or Supersoul. Because this transcendental position is at once achieved by one who is in Kṛṣṇa consciousness, the devotee of the Lord is unaffected by the dualities of material existence — distress and happiness, cold and heat, etc. This state is called *samādhi,* or absorption in the Supreme.

jñāna-vijñāna-tṛptātmā
kūṭa-stho vijitendriyaḥ

yukta ity ucyate yogī
sama-loṣṭrāśma-kāñcanaḥ

"A person is said to be established in self-realisation and is called a *yogī* [or mystic] when he is fully satisfied by virtue of acquired knowledge and realisation. Such a person is situated in transcendence and is self-controlled. He sees everything — whether it be pebbles, stones, or gold — as the same." (Bg. 6.8)

Book knowledge without realisation of the Supreme Truth is useless. This is stated as follows:

ataḥ śrī-kṛṣṇa-nāmādi
na bhaved grāhyam indriyaiḥ
sevonmukhe hi jihvādau
svayam eva sphuraty adaḥ

"No one can understand the transcendental nature of the name, form, quality, and pastimes of Śrī Kṛṣṇa through his materially contaminated senses. Only when one becomes spiritually saturated by transcendental service to the Lord are the transcendental name, form, quality and pastimes of the Lord revealed to him." (*Padma Purāṇa*)

There are men in the modes of goodness, passion and ignorance, and to reclaim all these conditioned souls, there are eighteen *Purāṇas.* Six *Purāṇas* are meant for those in the mode of goodness, six for those in the mode of passion and six for those in the mode of ignorance. The *Padma Purāṇa* is written for those in the mode of goodness. Because there are many different types of men, there are many different Vedic rituals. In the Vedic literatures there are descriptions of rituals and ceremonies in which a goat may be sacrificed in the presence of the goddess Kālī. This is described in the *Mārkaṇḍeya Purāṇa,* but this *Purāṇa* is meant for the instruction of those in the mode of ignorance.

It is very difficult for one to give up his attachments all at once. If one is addicted to meat-eating and is suddenly told that he must not eat meat, he cannot do so. If one is attached to drinking liquor and is suddenly told that liquor is no good, he cannot accept this advice. Therefore, in the *Purāṇas* we find certain instructions that say in essence, "All right, if you want to eat meat, just worship the goddess Kālī and sacrifice a goat for her. Only then can you eat meat. You cannot eat meat just by purchasing it from the butcher shop. No, there must be sacrifice or restriction." In order to sacrifice a goat to the goddess Kālī, one must make arrangements for a certain date and utilise certain paraphernalia. That type of *pūjā,* or worship, is allowed on the night of the dark moon, which means once a month. There are also certain *mantras* to be chanted when the goat is sacrificed. The goat is told, "Your life is being sacrificed before the goddess Kālī; you will therefore be immediately promoted to the human form." Generally, in order to attain the human form, a living entity has to pass through many species of life on the evolutionary scale, but if a goat is sacrificed to the goddess Kālī, he is immediately promoted to the human form. The *mantra* also says, "You have the right to kill this man who is sacrificing you." The word *māṁsa* indicates that in his next birth, the goat will eat the flesh of the man who is presently sacrificing him. This in itself should bring the goat-eater to his senses. He should consider, "Why am I eating this flesh? Why am I doing this? I'll have to repay with my own flesh in another life." The whole idea is to discourage one from eating meat.

Thus, because there are different types of men, there are eighteen *Purāṇas* to guide them. The Vedic literatures are meant to redeem all men, not just a few. It is not that those who are meat-eaters or drunkards are rejected. A doctor accepts all patients, and he prescribes different medicines according to the disease. It is not that he gives the same medicine for all diseases or that he treats just one disease. No, he offers a specific type of medicine to whomever comes, and the patient receives gradual treatment. However, the sattvic *Purāṇas* like the *Padma Purāṇa* are meant for those in the mode of goodness, for those who immediately are capable of worshiping the Supreme Personality of Godhead.

In *Brahma-saṁhitā* it is stated, *īśvaraḥ paramaḥ kṛṣṇaḥ sac-cid-ānanda-vigrahaḥ:* "The supreme controller is Kṛṣṇa, who has an eternal, blissful, spiritual body." This is the Vedic pronouncement, and we thus accept Śrī Kṛṣṇa as the Supreme Lord. Those who are in the modes of passion and ignorance attempt to imagine the form of God, and when they are confused, they say, "Oh, there is no personal God. God is impersonal, or void." This is just the result of frustration. Actually, God has His form. And why not? According to the *Vedānta-sūtra, janmādy asya yataḥ:* "The Supreme Absolute Truth is He from whom everything emanates." It is easy to see that we have different types of bodies, different types of forms. We must consider where these forms are coming from. Where have these forms originated? We have to use a little common sense. If God is not a person, how can His sons be persons? If your father is just a void, if he is not a person, how can you be a person? If your father has no form, how can you have form? This is not very difficult; it is just a common sense question. Unfortunately, because people are frustrated, they try to imagine some form, or they conclude that because this material form is temporary and troublesome, God must be formless. Indeed, because all forms in this material world must perish, God, of necessity, must be formless.

Brahma-saṁhitā specifically states that this conception is a mistake. *Īśvaraḥ paramaḥ kṛṣṇaḥ sac-cid-ānanda-vigrahaḥ.*

God has form, but His form is *sac-cid-ānanda-vigraha. Sat* means "eternal", *cit* means "knowledge" and *ānanda* means "pleasure". God has form, but His form is eternal and is full of knowledge and pleasure. We cannot compare His form to our form. Our form is neither eternal, full of pleasure, nor full of knowledge; therefore God's form is different.

As soon as we speak of form, we think that form must be like ours, and we therefore conclude that the eternal, all-knowing and all-blissful God must be without form. This is not knowledge but the result of imperfect speculation. According to *Padma Purāṇa, ataḥ śrī-kṛṣṇa-nāmādi na bhaved grāhyam indriyaiḥ:* "One cannot understand the form, name, quality or paraphernalia of God with one's material senses." Since our senses are imperfect, we cannot speculate on Him who is supremely perfect. That is not possible.

Then how is it possible to understand Him? *Sevonmukhe hi jihvādau.* By training and purifying our senses, we may come to understand and see God. Presently we are attempting to understand God with impure, imperfect senses. It is like someone with cataracts trying to see. Just because one has cataracts, he should not conclude that there is nothing to be seen. Similarly, we cannot presently conceive of God's form, but once our cataracts are removed, we can see. According to the *Brahma-saṁhitā, premāñjana-cchurita-bhakti-vilocanena santaḥ sadaiva hṛdayeṣu vilokayanti:* "The devotees whose eyes are anointed with the ointment of love of God can see God within their hearts twenty-four hours a day." Purification of the senses is what is required; then we can understand the name, form, qualities and pastimes of God. Then we'll be able to see God everywhere and in everything.

These matters are discussed thoroughly in the Vedic literatures. For instance, it is said that although God has no hands or legs, He can accept whatever we offer (*apāṇi-pādo javano gṛhītā*). It is also stated that although God has neither eyes nor ears, He can see and hear everything. These are apparent contradictions, but they are meant to teach us an important lesson. When we speak of seeing, we think of material vision. Due to our material conception, we think that the eyes of God must be like ours. Therefore, in order to remove these material conceptions, the Vedic literatures say that God has no hands, legs, eyes, ears, etc. God has eyes, but His vision is infinite. He can see in darkness, and He can see everywhere at once; therefore He has different eyes. Similarly, God has ears and can hear. He may be in His kingdom, millions and millions of miles away, but He can hear us whispering, because He is sitting within. We cannot avoid God's seeing, hearing or touching.

patraṁ puṣpaṁ phalaṁ toyaṁ
yo me bhaktyā prayacchati
tad ahaṁ bhakty-upahṛtam
aśnāmi prayatātmanaḥ

"If one offers Me with love and devotion a leaf, a flower, fruit or water, I will accept it." (Bg. 9.26) If God does not have senses, how can He accept and eat the offerings that are presented to Him? According to ritual, we are offering Kṛṣṇa food daily, and we can see that the taste of this food is immediately changed. This is a practical example. God eats, but because He is full, He does not eat like us. If I offer you a plate of food, you will eat it, and it will be finished. God is not hungry, but He eats, and at the same time, He leaves the food as it is, and thus it is transformed into *prasāda*, His mercy. *Pūrṇasya pūrṇam ādāya pūrṇam evāvaśiṣyate.* God is full, yet He accepts all the food that we offer. Still, the food remains as it is. He can eat with His eyes. As stated in *Brahma-saṁhitā, aṅgāni yasya sakalendriya-vṛtti-manti:* "Every sense of the Lord's body has all the potencies of the other senses." Although we can see with our eyes, we cannot eat with our eyes. The senses of God, however, being infinite, are different. Simply by looking at the food that is offered to Him, He eats it.

This may not be understood at the present moment; therefore the *Padma Purāṇa* states that when one becomes spiritually saturated by rendering transcendental service to the Lord, the transcendental name, form, qualities and pastimes of the Lord are revealed. We cannot understand God by our own endeavour, but out of mercy God reveals Himself to us. If it is night and you want to see the sun, you will have to wait for the sun to appear in the morning. You cannot go outside with a big torch and say, "Come on, I will show you the sunlight." In the morning, when the sun rises of its own will, we can see it. Because our senses are imperfect, we cannot see God by our own endeavour. We have to purify our senses and wait for the time when God will be pleased to reveal Himself to us. That is the process. We cannot challenge God. We cannot say, "O my dear God, my dear Kṛṣṇa. Please come. I want to see You." No, God is not our order-supplier. He is not our servant. When He is pleased, we will see Him; therefore this Kṛṣṇa consciousness is a process by which we can please God so that He will reveal Himself to us.

Because people cannot see God, they readily accept anyone who says, "I am God." Because people have no conception of God, they are eager to accept any rascal who comes along and proclaims himself to be God. People are fond of saying, "I am searching after the truth," but in order to search for the truth, we must know what the truth is. Otherwise, how can we search it out? If we want to purchase gold, we must at least theoretically know what gold is, otherwise we will be cheated. Consequently, having no conception of the truth or of God, people are being cheated by so many rascals who say, "I am God." In a society of rascals, one rascal accepts another rascal as God, and this is all the result of rascaldom. But all this has nothing to do with God. One has to qualify himself to see and understand God, and that process of qualification is called Kṛṣṇa consciousness. *Sevonmukhe hi jihvādau svayam eva sphuraty adaḥ:* by engaging ourselves in God's service, we become qualified to see God. Otherwise it is not possible. We may be great scientists or scholars, but our mundane scholarship will not help us see God.

This *Bhagavad-gītā* is the science of Kṛṣṇa consciousness, and in order to understand Kṛṣṇa, we must be fortunate enough to associate with a person who is in pure Kṛṣṇa consciousness. We cannot understand *Bhagavad-gītā* simply by acquiring an M.A., Ph.D., or whatever. *Bhagavad-gītā* is a transcendental science, and it requires different senses in order to be understood. Our senses must be purified by the rendering of service, not by the acquiring of academic degrees. There are many Ph.D.'s, many scholars, who cannot understand Kṛṣṇa. Therefore Kṛṣṇa appears in the material world. Although He is unborn (*ajo 'pi sann avyayātmā*), He comes to reveal Himself to us.

Thus Kṛṣṇa is realised by the grace of Kṛṣṇa or by the grace of a Kṛṣṇa conscious person who has realised Kṛṣṇa by the grace of Kṛṣṇa. We cannot understand Him through academic knowledge. We can only understand Kṛṣṇa by acquiring the grace of Kṛṣṇa. Once we acquire His grace, we can see Him, talk with Him—do whatever we desire. It is not that Kṛṣṇa is a void. He is a person, the Supreme Person, and we can have a relationship with Him. That is the Vedic injunction. *Nityo nityānāṁ cetanaś cetanānām:* "We are all eternal persons, and God is the supreme eternal person." We are all eternal, and God is the supreme eternal. Presently, because we are encaged within these bodies, we are experiencing birth and death, but actually we are beyond birth and death. We are eternal spirit souls, but according to our work and desires, we are transmigrating from one body to another. It is explained in the Second Chapter of *Bhagavad-gītā* (2.20),

na jāyate mriyate vā kadācin
nāyaṁ bhūtvā bhavitā vā na bhūyaḥ
ajo nityaḥ śāśvato 'yaṁ purāṇo
na hanyate hanyamāne śarīre

"For the soul there is neither birth nor death at any time. He has not come into being, does not come into being, and will not come into being. He is unborn, eternal, ever-existing and primeval. He is not slain when the body is slain."

Just as God is eternal, we are also eternal, and when we establish our eternal relationship with the supreme, complete eternal, we realise our eternality. *Nityo nityānāṁ cetanaś cetanānām.* God is the supreme living entity among all living entities, the supreme eternal among all eternals. By Kṛṣṇa consciousness, by purification of the senses, this knowledge will be realised, and we will come to see God.

A Kṛṣṇa conscious person has realised knowledge, by the grace of Kṛṣṇa, because he is satisfied with pure devotional service. By realised knowledge, one becomes perfect. By transcendental knowledge one can remain steady in his convictions, but by mere academic knowledge one can be easily deluded and confused by apparent contradictions. It is the realised soul who is actually self-controlled, because he is surrendered to Kṛṣṇa. He is transcendental because he has nothing to do with mundane scholarship. For him, mundane scholarship and mental speculation, which may be as good as gold to others, are of no greater value than pebbles or stones.

Even if one is illiterate, he can realise God simply by engaging himself in submissive, transcendental loving service. God is not subjected to any material condition. He is supreme spirit, and the process of realising Him is also beyond material considerations. Therefore, one may be a very learned scholar and still not be able to understand God. One should not think that because he is very poor he cannot realise God; nor should one think that he can realise God just because he is very rich. God may be understood by an uneducated person and misunderstood by one with great education. The understanding of God, like God Himself, is unconditional (*apratihata*).

In *Śrīmad-Bhāgavatam* (1.2.6) it is stated,

sa vai puṁsāṁ paro dharmo
yato bhaktir adhokṣaje
ahaituky apratihatā
yayātmā suprasīdati

"The supreme occupation (*dharma*) for all humanity is that by which men can attain to loving devotional service unto the transcendent Lord. Such devotional service must be unmotivated and uninterrupted to completely satisfy the self." Cultivation of love of God: that is the definition of first-class religion. Just as there are three *guṇas,* or three qualities, in the material world, there are various religions, each situated in one of the three modes. We are not, however, concerned with analysing these religious conceptions. For us, the purpose of religion is to understand God and to learn how to love God. That is the real purpose of any first-class religious system. If a religion does not teach love of God, it is useless. One may follow his religious principles very carefully, but if one does not possess love of God, his religion is null and void. According to *Śrīmad-Bhāgavatam* (1.2.6) real religion must be *ahaitukī* and *apratihatā:* without selfish motivation and without impediment. By practising such a religion, we will become happy in all respects.

Sa vai puṁsāṁ paro dharmo yato bhaktir adhokṣaje. Another name for God is *adhokṣaja,* which means "one who cannot be seen by materialistic attempts". That is to say that God conquers all our attempts to see Him materially. The word *akṣaja* refers to experimental knowledge, and *adhaḥ* means "unreachable". So God cannot be reached through experimental knowledge. We have to learn to contact Him in a different way: through submissive hearing and the rendering of transcendental loving service.

True religion teaches causeless love of God. It does not say, "I love God because He supplies me nice objects for my sense gratification." That is not love. God is great, God is our eternal father, and it is our duty to love Him. There is no question of barter or exchange. We should not think, "Oh, God gives me my daily bread; therefore I love God." God gives daily bread even to the cats and dogs. Since He is the father of everyone, He is supplying everyone food. So loving God for daily bread is not love. Love is without reason. Even if God does not supply us our daily bread, we should love Him. That is true love. As Caitanya Mahāprabhu said, *āśliṣya vā pāda-ratāṁ pinaṣṭu mām adarśanān marma-hatāṁ karotu vā:* "I know no one but Kṛṣṇa as my Lord, and He shall remain so even if He handles me roughly by His embrace or makes me broken-hearted by not being present before me. He is completely free to do anything and everything, for He is always my worshipful Lord, unconditionally." That is the sentiment of one who is established in pure love of God. When we attain that stage of love of God, we will find that everything is full of pleasure; God is full of pleasure, and we also are full of pleasure.

suhṛn-mitrāry-udāsīna-
madhyastha-dveṣya-bandhuṣu
sādhuṣv api ca pāpeṣu
sama-buddhir viśiṣyate

"A person is considered still further advanced when he regards honest well-wishers, affectionate benefactors, the neutral, mediators, the envious, friends and enemies, the pious and the sinners all with an equal mind." (Bg. 6.9) This is a sign of real spiritual advancement. In this material world we are considering people friends and enemies on the bodily platform — that is, on the basis of sense gratification. If one gratifies our senses, he is our friend, and if he doesn't, he is our enemy. However, once we have realised God, or the Absolute Truth, there are no such material considerations.

In this material world, all conditioned souls are under illusion. A doctor treats all patients, and although a patient may be delirious and insult the doctor, the doctor does not refuse to treat him. He still administers the medicine that is required. As Lord Jesus Christ said, we should hate the sin, not the sinner. That is a very nice statement, because the sinner is under illusion. He is mad. If we hate him, how can we deliver him? Therefore, those who are advanced devotees, who are really servants of God, do not hate anyone. When Lord Jesus Christ was being crucified, he said, "My God, forgive them. They know not what they do." This is the proper attitude of an advanced devotee. He understands that the conditioned souls cannot be hated, because they have become mad due to their materialistic way of thinking. In this Kṛṣṇa consciousness movement, there is no question of hating anyone. Everyone is welcomed to come and chant Hare Kṛṣṇa, take *kṛṣṇa-prasādam*, listen to the philosophy of *Bhagavad-gītā,* and try to rectify material, conditioned life. This is the essential programme of Kṛṣṇa consciousness. Therefore, Lord Caitanya Mahāprabhu said,

yāre dekha, tāre kaha 'kṛṣṇa'-upadeśa
āmāra ājñāya guru hañā tāra' ei deśa

"Instruct everyone to follow the orders of Lord Śrī Kṛṣṇa as they are given in *Bhagavad-gītā* and *Śrīmad-Bhāgavatam.* In this way become a spiritual master and try to liberate everyone in this land." (Cc. *Madhya* 7.128).

yogī yuñjīta satatam
ātmānaṁ rahasi sthitaḥ
ekākī yata-cittātmā
nirāśīr aparigrahaḥ

"A transcendentalist should always engage his body, mind and self in relationship with the Supreme; he should live alone in a secluded place and should always carefully control his mind. He should be free from desires and feelings of possessiveness." (Bg. 6.10)

In this chapter, in which the Lord is teaching the principles of the *yoga* system, He here points out that a transcendentalist should always try to concentrate his mind on the Supreme Self. "The Supreme Self" refers to Kṛṣṇa, the Supreme Lord. As explained before (*nityo nityānāṁ cetanaś cetanānām*), God is the supreme eternal, the supreme living entity, the Supreme Self. The purpose of the entire *yoga* system is to concentrate the mind on this Supreme Self. We are not the Supreme Self. That should be understood. The Supreme Self is God. This is *dvaita-vāda* — duality. Duality means that God is different from me. He is supreme, and I am subordinate. He is great, and I am small. He is infinite, and I am infinitesimal. This is the relationship between ourselves and God as we should understand it. Because we are infinitesimal, we should concentrate our mind on the infinite Supreme Self. In order to do this, we should live alone, and "living alone" means that we should not live with those who are not Kṛṣṇa conscious. Ideally, this means that one should live in a secluded place, like a forest or a jungle, but in this age such a secluded place is very difficult to find. Therefore "secluded place" refers to that place where God consciousness is taught.

The transcendentalist should also carefully control his mind, and this means fixing the mind on the Supreme Self, or Kṛṣṇa. As explained before, Kṛṣṇa is just like the sun, and if the mind is fixed on Him, there is no question of darkness. If Kṛṣṇa is always on our minds, *māyā,* or illusion, can never enter. This is the process of concentration.

The transcendentalist should also be free from desires and feelings of possessiveness. People are materially diseased because they desire things and want to possess them. We desire that which we do not have, and we lament for that which we have lost. *Brahma-bhūtaḥ prasannātmā.* One who is actually God conscious does not desire material possessions. He has only one desire — to serve Kṛṣṇa. It is not possible to give up desire, but it *is* possible to purify our desires. It is the nature of the living entity to have some desire, but in the conditioned state, one's desire is contaminated. Conditioned, one thinks, "I desire to satisfy my senses by material possession." Purified desire is desire for Kṛṣṇa, and if we desire Kṛṣṇa, desires for material possessions will automatically vanish.

śucau deśe pratiṣṭhāpya
sthiram āsanam ātmanaḥ
nāty-ucchritaṁ nāti-nīcaṁ
cailājina-kuśottaram

tatraikāgraṁ manaḥ kṛtvā
yata-cittendriya-kriyaḥ
upaviśyāsane yuñjyād
yogam ātma-viśuddhaye

"To practise *yoga,* one should go to a secluded place and should lay *kuśa* grass on the ground and then cover it with a deerskin and a soft cloth. The seat should be neither too high nor too low and should be situated in a sacred place. The *yogī* should then sit on it very firmly and practise *yoga* to purify the heart by controlling the mind, senses and activities and fixing the mind on one point." (Bg. 6.11-12). In these verses it is emphasised how and where one should sit. In the United Kingdom and other Western countries, there are many so-called *yoga* societies, but they do not practise *yoga* according to these prescriptions. "A sacred place" refers to a place of pilgrimage. In India, the *yogīs,* the transcendentalists, or devotees, all leave home and reside in sacred places such as Prayāga, Mathurā, Vṛndāvana, Hṛṣīkeśa, and Hardwar and in solitude practise *yoga* where the sacred rivers like the Yamunā and the Ganges flow. So how is this possible in this age? How many people are prepared to find such a sacred place? In order to earn one's livelihood, one has to live in a congested city. There is no question of finding a sacred place, but for the practice of *yoga,* that is the first prerequisite.

Therefore in this *bhakti-yoga* system, the temple is considered the sacred place. The temple is *nirguṇa* — transcendental. According to the *Vedas*, a city is in the mode of passion, and a forest is in the mode of goodness. The temple, however, is transcendental. If you live in a city or town, you live in a place where passion is predominant, and if you want to escape this, you may go to a forest, a place of goodness. God's temple, however, is above passion and goodness; therefore the temple of Kṛṣṇa is the only secluded place for this age. In this age, it is not possible to retreat to a forest; nor is it useful to make a show of practising *yoga* in so-called *yoga* societies and at the same time engage in nonsense.

Therefore, in the *Bṛhan-nāradīya Purāṇa* it is said that in Kali-yuga, when people are generally short-lived, slow in spiritual realisation, and always disturbed by various anxieties, the best means of spiritual realisation is chanting the holy names of the Lord.

harer nāma harer nāma
harer nāmaiva kevalam
kalau nāsty eva nāsty eva
nāsty eva gatir anyathā

"In this age of quarrel and hypocrisy, the only means of deliverance is chanting the holy name of the Lord. There is no other way. There is no other way. There is no other way."

This is the solution, the grand gift of Caitanya Mahāprabhu. In this age, other *yoga* practices are not feasible, but this practice is so simple and universal that even a child can take to it.

CHAPTER FOUR

Moderation in Yoga

In this Sixth Chapter of *Bhagavad-gītā*, the system of *sāṅkhya-yoga,* which is the meditational *aṣṭāṅga-yoga* system, is emphasised. *Jñāna-yoga* emphasises the philosophical process of analysis by which we determine what is Brahman and what is not Brahman. This process is known as the *neti neti* process, or "not this, not that". In the beginning of the *Vedānta-sūtra* it is stated, *janmādy asya yataḥ:* "The Supreme Brahman, the Absolute Truth, is He from whom everything emanates." This is a hint, and from this we must try to understand the nature of the Supreme Brahman, from whom everything is emanating. The nature of that Absolute Truth is explained in detail in *Śrīmad-Bhāgavatam.*

In the first verse of *Śrīmad-Bhāgavatam* it is stated,

oṁ namo bhagavate vāsudevāya
janmādy asya yato 'nvayād itarataś cārtheṣv abhijñaḥ svarāṭ
tene brahma hṛdā ya ādi-kavaye muhyanti yat sūrayaḥ
tejo-vāri-mṛdāṁ yathā vinimayo yatra tri-sargo 'mṛṣā
dhāmnā svena sadā nirasta-kuhakaṁ satyaṁ paraṁ dhīmahi

"O my Lord, Śrī Kṛṣṇa, son of Vasudeva, O all-pervading Personality of Godhead, I offer my respectful obeisances unto You. I meditate upon Lord Śrī Kṛṣṇa because He is the

Absolute Truth and the primeval cause of all causes of the creation, sustenance and destruction of the manifested universes. He is directly and indirectly conscious of all manifestations, and He is independent because there is no other cause beyond Him. It is He only who first imparted the Vedic knowledge unto the heart of Brahmājī, the original living being. By Him even the great sages and demigods are placed into illusion, as one is bewildered by the illusory representations of water seen in fire, or land seen on water. Only because of Him do the material universes, temporarily manifested by the reactions of the three modes of nature, appear factual, although they are unreal. I therefore meditate upon Him, Lord Śrī Kṛṣṇa, who is eternally existent in the transcendental abode which is forever free from the illusory representations of the material world. I meditate upon Him, for He is the Absolute Truth."

Thus from the very beginning of *Śrīmad-Bhāgavatam* the Absolute Truth is proclaimed to be cognizant. He is not dead or void. And what is the nature of His cognizance? *Anvayād itarataś cārtheṣu:* "He is directly and indirectly cognizant of all manifestations." To a limited degree, each and every living entity is cognizant, but we are not completely cognizant. I may claim, "This is my head," but if someone asks me, "Do you know how many hairs are on your head?" I will not be able to reply. Of course, this kind of knowledge is not transcendental, but in *Śrīmad-Bhāgavatam* it is stated that the Supreme Absolute Truth knows everything, directly and indirectly. I may know that I am eating, but I do not know the intricacies of the eating process—how my body is exactly assimilating food, how the blood is passing through my veins, etc. I am cognizant that my body is functioning, but I do not know how these processes are working perfectly and all at once. This is because my knowledge is limited.

By definition, God is He who knows everything. He knows what is going on in every corner of His creation; therefore, from the very beginning, *Śrīmad-Bhāgavatam* explains that the Supreme Truth from whom everything is emanating is supremely cognizant (*abhijñaḥ*). One may ask, "If the Absolute Truth is so powerful, wise and cognizant, He must have attained this knowledge from some similar being." This is not the case. If He attains His knowledge from someone else, He is not God. *Svarāṭ.* He is independent, and His knowledge is automatically there.

Śrīmad-Bhāgavatam is the supreme combination of both the *jñāna-* and *bhakti-yoga* systems, because it analyses in detail the nature of that Supreme Being from whom everything is emanating. By the *jñāna-yoga* system, one attempts to understand the nature of the Absolute Truth in a philosophical way. In the *bhakti-yoga* system, the target is the same. The methodology, however, is somewhat different. Whereas the *jñānī* attempts to concentrate his mind philosophically on the Supreme, the *bhakta* simply engages himself in the service of the Supreme Lord, and the Lord reveals Himself. The *jñāna* method is called the ascending process, and the *bhakti* method is called the descending process. If we are in the darkness of night, we may attempt to attain the sunlight by ascending in a powerful rocket. According to the descending process, however, we simply await the sunrise, and then we understand immediately.

Through the ascending process, we attempt to reach the Supreme through our own endeavour, through the process of induction. By induction, we may attempt to find out whether man is mortal by studying thousands of men, trying to see whether they are mortal or immortal. This, of course, will take a great deal of time. If, however, I accept from superior authority the fact that all men are mortal, my knowledge is complete and immediate. Thus it is stated in *Śrīmad-Bhāgavatam* (10.14.29), "My dear Lord, a person who has received a little favour from You can understand You very quickly. But those who are trying to understand You by the ascending process may go on speculating for millions of years and still never understand You."

By mental speculation, one is more likely to simply reach a point of frustration and confusion and conclude, "Oh, God is zero." But if God is zero, how are so many figures emanating from Him? As the *Vedānta* says (*janmādy asya yataḥ*), "Everything is generating from the Supreme." Therefore the Supreme cannot be zero. We have to study how so many forms, so many infinite living entities, are being generated from the Supreme. This is also explained in the *Vedānta-sūtra,* which is the study of ultimate knowledge. The word *veda* means "knowledge", and *anta* means "ultimate". Ultimate knowledge is knowledge of the Supreme Lord.

So how is it possible to understand the form of Kṛṣṇa? If it is stated that God does not have eyes, limbs, and senses like ours, how are we to understand His transcendental senses, His transcendental form? This is not possible by mental speculation. We simply have to serve Him, and then He will reveal Himself to us. As Kṛṣṇa Himself states in the Tenth Chapter of *Bhagavad-gītā* (10.11),

teṣām evānukampārtham
aham ajñāna-jaṁ tamaḥ
nāśayāmy ātma-bhāva-stho
jñāna-dīpena bhāsvatā

"To show them special mercy, I, dwelling in their hearts, destroy with the shining lamp of knowledge the darkness born of ignorance." Kṛṣṇa is within us, and when we are sincerely searching for Him by the devotional process, He will reveal Himself.

Again, as stated in the Eighteenth Chapter of *Bhagavad-gītā* (18.55),

bhaktyā mām abhijānāti
yāvān yaś cāsmi tattvataḥ
tato māṁ tattvato jñātvā
viśate tad-anantaram

"One can understand Me as I am, as the Supreme Personality of Godhead, only by devotional service. And when one is in full consciousness of Me by such devotion, he can enter into the kingdom of God." Thus God has to be understood by this process of *bhakti-yoga,* which is the process of *śravaṇaṁ kīrtanaṁ viṣṇoḥ* — hearing and chanting about Viṣṇu. This is the beginning of the *bhakti-yoga* process. If we but hear sincerely and submissively, we will understand. Kṛṣṇa will reveal Himself. *Śravaṇaṁ kīrtanaṁ viṣṇoḥ smaraṇaṁ pāda-sevanam arcanaṁ vandanaṁ dāsyam.* There are nine different processes in the *bhakti-yoga* system. By *vandanam,* we offer prayers, and that is also *bhakti. Śravaṇam* is hearing about Kṛṣṇa from *Bhagavad-gītā, Śrīmad-Bhāgavatam* and other *śāstras. Kīrtanam* is chanting about His glories, chanting the Hare Kṛṣṇa *mantra.* This is the beginning of the *bhakti-yoga* process. *Śravaṇaṁ kīrtanaṁ viṣṇoḥ.* Everything is Viṣṇu, and meditation is on Viṣṇu. It is not possible to have *bhakti* without Viṣṇu. Kṛṣṇa is the original form of Viṣṇu (*kṛṣṇas tu bhagavān svayam:* "Kṛṣṇa is the original form of the Supreme Personality of Godhead"). If we but follow this *bhakti-yoga* process, we should be able to understand the Supreme, and all doubts should be removed.

The *aṣṭāṅga-yoga* process is outlined very specifically in the Sixth Chapter of *Bhagavad-gītā* (6.13-14):

samaṁ kāya-śiro-grīvaṁ
dhārayann acalaṁ sthiraḥ

samprekṣya nāsikāgraṁ svaṁ
diśaś cānavalokayan

praśāntātmā vigata-bhīr
brahmacāri-vrate sthitaḥ
manaḥ saṁyamya mac-citto
yukta āsīta mat-paraḥ

"One should hold one's body, neck and head erect in a straight line and stare steadily at the tip of the nose. Thus, with an unagitated, subdued mind, devoid of fear, completely free from sex life, one should meditate upon Me within the heart and make Me the ultimate goal of life." *Yoga* does not mean going to some class, paying a fee, engaging in gymnastics and then returning home to drink, smoke and engage in sex. Such *yoga* is practised by societies of the cheaters and the cheated. The authoritative *yoga* system is here outlined by the supreme authority, Śrī Kṛṣṇa Himself. Is there a better *yogī* than Kṛṣṇa, the Supreme Personality of Godhead? First of all, one has to go alone to a holy place and sit in a straight line, holding one's body, neck and head erect, and stare steadily at the tip of the nose. Why is this? This is a method to help concentrate one's mind. That's all. The real purpose of *yoga,* however, is to keep oneself always aware that Lord Kṛṣṇa is within.

One of the dangers of sitting in meditation and staring at the tip of one's nose is that one will fall asleep. I have seen many so-called meditators sitting like this and snoring. As soon as one closes his eyes, it is natural to feel sleepy; therefore it is recommended that the eyes are half closed. Thus it is said that one should look at the tip of his nose. With one's sight thus concentrated, the mind should be subdued and unagitated. In India, the *yogī* often goes to a jungle to practise such meditation in solitude. But in a jungle, the *yogī* may think, "Maybe some tiger or snake is coming. What is that noise?" In this way, his mind may be agitated; therefore it is especially stated that the *yogī* must be "devoid of fear". A deerskin is especially recommended as a *yoga-āsana,* because it contains a chemical property that repels snakes; thus the *yogī* will not be disturbed by serpents. Whatever the case — serpents, tigers or lions — one can be truly fearless only when he is established in Kṛṣṇa consciousness. Due to perverted memory, the conditioned soul is naturally fearful. Fear is due to forgetting one's eternal relationship with Kṛṣṇa. According to *Śrīmad-Bhāgavatam* (11.2.37): *bhayaṁ dvitīyābhiniveśataḥ syād īśād apetasya viparyayo 'smṛtiḥ.* Kṛṣṇa consciousness provides the only true basis for fearlessness; therefore perfect practise of *yoga* is not possible for one who is not Kṛṣṇa conscious.

The *yogī* must also be "completely free from sex life". If one indulges in sex, he cannot concentrate; therefore *brahmacarya,* complete celibacy, is recommended to make the mind steady. By practising celibacy, one cultivates determination. One modern example of such determination is that of Mahatma Gandhi, who was determined to resist the powerful British empire by means of nonviolence. At this time, India was dependent on the British, and the people had no weapons. The Britishers, being more powerful, easily cut down whatever violent revolutions the people attempted. Therefore Gandhi resorted to nonviolence, noncooperation. "I shall not fight with the Britishers," he declared, "and even if they react with violence, I shall remain nonviolent. In this way the world will sympathise with us." Such a policy required a great amount of determination, and Gandhi's determination was very strong because he was a *brahmacārī.* Although he had children and a wife, he renounced sex at the age of thirty-six. It was this sexual renunciation that enabled him to be so determined that he was able to lead his country and drive the British from India.

Thus, refraining from sex enables one to be very determined and powerful. It is not necessary to do anything else. This is a secret people are not aware of. If you want to do something with determination, you have to refrain from sex. Regardless of the process — be it *haṭha-yoga, bhakti-yoga, jñāna-yoga* or whatever — sex indulgence is not allowed. Sex is allowed only for householders who want to beget good children and raise them in Kṛṣṇa consciousness. Sex is not meant for sense enjoyment, although enjoyment is there by nature. Unless there is some enjoyment, why should one assume the responsibility of begetting children? That is the secret of nature's gift, but we should not take advantage of it. These are the secrets of life. By taking advantage and indulging in sex life, we are simply wasting our time. If one tells you that you can indulge in sex as much as you like and at the same time become a *yogī*, he is cheating you. If some so-called *guru* tells you to give him money in exchange for some *mantra* and that you can go on and engage in all kinds of nonsense, he is just cheating you. Because we want something sublime and yet want it cheaply, we put ourselves in a position to be cheated. This means that we actually want to be cheated. If we want something valuable, we must pay for it. We cannot expect to walk into a jewellery store and demand the most valuable jewel for a mere ten pence. No, we must pay a great deal. Similarly, if we want perfection in *yoga*, we have to pay by abstaining from sex. Perfection in *yoga* is not something childish, and *Bhagavad-gītā* instructs us that if we try to make *yoga* into something childish, we will be cheated. There are many cheaters awaiting us, waiting to take our money, giving us nothing and then leaving. But according to Śrī Kṛṣṇa's authoritative statement in *Bha-*

gavad-gītā, one must be "completely free from sex life". Being free from sex, one should "meditate upon Me within the heart and make Me the ultimate goal of life". This is real meditation.

Kṛṣṇa does not recommend meditation on the void. He specifically states, "meditate upon Me". The *viṣṇu-mūrti* is situated in one's heart, and meditation upon Him is the object of *yoga*. This is the *sāṅkhya-yoga* system, as first practised by Lord Kapiladeva, an incarnation of God. By sitting straight, staring steadily at the tip of one's nose, subduing one's mind and abstaining from sex, one may be able to concentrate the mind on the *viṣṇu-mūrti* situated within the heart. When we refer to the Viṣṇu form, or *viṣṇu-mūrti*, we refer to Śrī Kṛṣṇa.

In this Kṛṣṇa consciousness movement we are meditating directly on Śrī Kṛṣṇa. This is a process of practical meditation. The members of this movement are concentrating their minds on Kṛṣṇa, regardless of their particular occupation. One may be working in the garden and digging in the earth, but he is thinking, "I am cultivating beautiful roses to offer to Kṛṣṇa." One may be cooking in the kitchen, but he is always thinking, "I am preparing palatable food to be offered to Kṛṣṇa." Similarly, chanting and dancing in the temple are forms of meditating on Kṛṣṇa. Thus the boys and girls in this society for Kṛṣṇa consciousness are perfect *yogīs* because they are meditating on Kṛṣṇa twenty-four hours a day. We are teaching the perfect *yoga* system, not according to our personal whims but according to the authority of *Bhagavad-gītā*. Nothing is concocted or manufactured. The verses of *Bhagavad-gītā* are there for all to see. The activities of the *bhakti-yogīs* in this movement are so moulded that the practitioners cannot help but think of Kṛṣṇa at all times. "Meditate upon Me within the heart, and make Me the ultimate goal of life," Śrī Kṛṣṇa says. This is the perfect *yoga* system, and one who practises it prepares himself to be transferred to Kṛṣṇaloka.

yuñjann evaṁ sadātmānaṁ
yogī niyata-mānasaḥ
śāntiṁ nirvāṇa-paramāṁ
mat-saṁsthām adhigacchati

"Thus practising control of the body, mind and activities, the mystic transcendentalist, his mind regulated, attains to the kingdom of God [or the abode of Kṛṣṇa] by cessation of material existence." (Bg. 6.15)

It is stated in Sanskrit in this verse, *śāntiṁ nirvāṇa-paramām;* that is, one attains peace through *nirvāṇa-paramām*, or the cessation of material activities. *Nirvāṇa* does not refer to void, but to putting an end to materialistic activities. Unless one puts an end to them, there is no question of peace. When Hiraṇyakaśipu asked his five-year-old son Prahlāda Mahārāja, "My dear boy, what is the best thing you have thus far learned?" Prahlāda immediately replied, *tat sādhu manye 'sura-varya dehināṁ sadā samudvigna-dhiyām asad-grahāt:* "My dear father, O greatest of the demons, materialistic people are always full of anxiety because they have accepted as real that which is nonpermanent." The word *asad-grahāt* is important because it indicates that materialists are always hankering to capture or possess something that is nonpermanent. History affords us many examples. Mr. Kennedy was a very rich man who wanted to become President, and he spent a great deal of money to attain that elevated position. Yet although he had a nice wife, children and the presidency, everything was finished within a second. In the material world, people are always trying to capture something that is nonpermanent. Unfortunately, people do not come to their senses and realise, "I am permanent. I am spirit soul. Why am I hankering after something that is non-permanent?"

We are always busy acquiring comforts for this body without considering that today, tomorrow or in a hundred years this body will be finished. As far as the real "I" is concerned, "I am spirit soul. I have no birth. I have no death. What, then, is my proper function?" When we act on the material platform, we are engaged in bodily functions; therefore Prahlāda Mahārāja says that people are anxious because all their activities are targeted to capturing and possessing something nonpermanent. All living entities — men, beasts, birds or whatever — are always full of anxiety, and this is the material disease. If we are always full of anxiety, how can we attain peace? People may live in a very nice house, but out front they place signs saying, "Beware of Dog", or "No Trespassers". This means that although they are living comfortably, they are anxious that someone will come to molest them. Sitting in an office and earning a very good salary, a man is always thinking, "Oh, I hope I don't lose this position." The British nation is very rich, but because of this, it has to maintain a great defence force. So who is free from anxiety? The conclusion is that if we want peace without anxiety, we have to come to Kṛṣṇa consciousness. There is no alternative.

In order to attain peace, we must meditate on Kṛṣṇa, and by meditating on Kṛṣṇa, we can control the body. The first part of the body to control is the tongue, and the next part is the genital. When these are controlled, everything is controlled. The tongue is controlled by chanting and eating *kṛṣṇa-prasādam.* As soon as the tongue is controlled, the stomach is controlled, and next the genitals are controlled. Actually, controlling the body and mind is a very simple process. When the mind is fixed on Kṛṣṇa and has no other engagement, it is automatically controlled. Activities should always be centred on working for Kṛṣṇa — gardening, typing, cooking, cleaning, whatever. By engaging the body, mind and activities in the service of Kṛṣṇa, one attains the supreme *nirvāṇa,* which abides in Kṛṣṇa. Everything is in Kṛṣṇa; therefore we cannot find peace outside Kṛṣṇa conscious activities.

The ultimate goal of *yoga* is thus clearly explained. *Yoga* is not meant for attaining any kind of material facility; it is to enable the cessation of all material existence. As long as we require some material facilities, we will get them. But these facilities will not solve the problems of life. I have travelled throughout the world, and it is my opinion that Western boys and girls have the best material facilities, but does this mean that they have attained peace? Can anyone say, "Yes, I am completely peaceful"? If this is so, why are Western youngsters so frustrated and confused?

As long as we practise *yoga* in order to attain some material facility, there will be no question of peace. *Yoga* should only be practised in order to understand Kṛṣṇa. *Yoga* is meant for the reestablishment of our lost relationship with Kṛṣṇa. Generally, one joins a *yoga* society in order to improve his health, to reduce fat. People in rich nations eat more, become fat and then pay exorbitant prices to so-called *yoga* instructors in order to reduce. People try to reduce by all these artificial gymnastics; they do not understand that if they just eat vegetables or fruits and grains, they will never get fat. People get fat because they eat voraciously, because they eat meat. People who eat voraciously suffer from diabetes, overweight, heart attacks, etc., and those who eat insufficiently suffer from tuberculosis. Therefore moderation is required, and moderation in eating means that we eat only what is needed to keep body and soul together. If we eat more than we need or less, we will become diseased. All this is explained in the following verses:

nāty-aśnatas tu yogo 'sti
na caikāntam anaśnataḥ
na cāti-svapna-śīlasya
jāgrato naiva cārjuna

"There is no possibility of one's becoming a *yogī*, O Arjuna, if one eats too much or eats too little, sleeps too much or does not sleep enough." (Bg. 6.16)

yuktāhāra-vihārasya
yukta-ceṣṭasya karmasu
yukta-svapnāvabodhasya
yogo bhavati duḥkha-hā

"He who is regulated in his habits of eating, sleeping, recreation and work can mitigate all material pains by practising the *yoga* system." (Bg. 6.17) It is not that we are to starve ourselves. The body must be kept fit for any practice; therefore eating is required, and according to our programme, we eat only *kṛṣṇa-prasādam.* If you can comfortably eat ten pounds of food a day, then eat it, but if you try to eat ten pounds out of greed or avarice, you will suffer.

So in the practice of Kṛṣṇa consciousness, all these activities are present, but they are spiritualised. The cessation of material existence does not mean entering into "the void", which is only a myth. There is no void anywhere within the creation of the Lord. I am not void but spirit soul. If I were void, how would my bodily development take place? Where is this "void"? If we sow a seed in the ground, it grows into a plant or large tree. The father injects a seed into the womb of the mother, the body grows like a tree. Where is there void? In the Fourteenth Chapter of *Bhagavad-gītā* (14.4), Śrī Kṛṣṇa states,

sarva-yoniṣu kaunteya
mūrtayaḥ sambhavanti yāḥ
tāsāṁ brahma mahad yonir
ahaṁ bīja-pradaḥ pitā

"It should be understood that all species of life, O son of Kuntī, are made possible by birth in this material nature, and that I am the seed-giving father." The seed is originally given by Kṛṣṇa, placed in the womb of material nature, and thus many living entities are generated. How can one argue against this process? If the seed of existence is void, how has this body developed?

Nirvāṇa actually means not accepting another material body. It's not that we attempt to make this body void. *Nirvāṇa* means making the miserable, material, conditional body void — that is, converting the material body into a spiritual body. This means entering into the kingdom of God, which is described in the Fifteenth Chapter of *Bhagavad-gītā* (15.6):

na tad bhāsayate sūryo
sa śaśāṅko na pāvakaḥ
yad gatvā na nivartante
tad dhāma paramaṁ mama

"That abode of Mine is not illumined by the sun or moon, nor by fire or electricity. Those who reach it never return to this material world."

So there is no void anywhere within the Lord's creation. All the planets in the spiritual sky are self-illumined, like the sun. The kingdom of God is everywhere, but the spiritual sky and the planets thereof are all *paraṁ dhāma*, or superior abodes. As stated, sunlight, moonlight or electricity are not required in the *paraṁ dhāma*. We cannot find such an abode within this universe. We may travel as far as possible within our spaceships, but we will not find any place where there is no sunlight. The sunlight is so extensive that it pervades the universe. Therefore, that abode in which there is no sunlight, moonlight or electricity is beyond this material sky. Beyond this material nature is a spiritual nature. Actually, we know nothing of this material nature; we do not even know how it was originally formed. So how can we know anything about the spiritual nature beyond? We have to learn from Kṛṣṇa, who lives there; otherwise we remain in ignorance.

In this *Bhagavad-gītā*, information of the spiritual sky is given. How can we know anything about that which we cannot reach? Our senses are so imperfect, how can we attain knowledge? We just have to hear and accept. How will we ever know who our father is unless we accept the word of our mother? Our mother says, "Here is your father," and we have to accept this. We cannot determine our father by making enquiries here and there or by attempting to experiment. This knowledge is beyond our means. Similarly, if we want to learn about the spiritual sky, God's kingdom, we have to hear from the authority, mother *Vedas*. The *Vedas* are called *veda-mātā*, or mother *Vedas*, because the knowledge imparted therein is like that knowledge received from the mother. We *have* to believe in order to acquire knowledge. There is no possibility of acquiring this transcendental knowledge by experimenting with our imperfect senses.

A consummate *yogī*, who is perfect in understanding Lord Kṛṣṇa, as is clearly stated herein (*śāntiṁ nirvāṇa-paramāṁ mat-saṁsthām adhigacchati*) by the Lord Himself, can attain real peace and ultimately reach the supreme abode of the Lord. This abode is known as Kṛṣṇaloka, or Goloka Vṛndāvana. In *Brahma-saṁhitā* it is clearly stated (*goloka eva nivasaty akhilātma-bhūtaḥ*) that the Lord, although residing always in His abode called Goloka, is the all-pervading Brahman and the localised Paramātmā as well, by dint of His superior spiritual energies. No one can reach the spiritual sky or enter into the eternal abode of the Lord (Vaikuṇṭha, Goloka Vṛndāvana) without properly understanding Kṛṣṇa and His plenary expansion Viṣṇu. And according to *Brahma-saṁhitā,* it is necessary to learn from our authorised mother, *veda-mātā. Brahma-saṁhitā* states that the Supreme Lord is living not only in His abode, Goloka Vṛndāvana, but everywhere: *goloka eva nivasaty akhilātma-bhūtaḥ.* He is like the sun, which is millions of miles away and yet is still present within this room.

In summary, the person who works in Kṛṣṇa consciousness is the perfect *yogī,* because his mind is always absorbed in Kṛṣṇa's activities. *Sa vai manaḥ kṛṣṇa-padāravindayoḥ.* In the *Vedas* we also learn, *tam eva viditvāti mṛtyum eti:* "One can overcome the path of birth and death only by understanding the Supreme Personality of Godhead, Kṛṣṇa." Thus perfection of *yoga* is the attainment of freedom from material existence and not some magical jugglery or gymnastic feat to befool innocent people.

In this system of *yoga,* moderation is required; therefore it is stated that we should not eat too much or too little, sleep too much or too little, or work too much or too little. All these activities are there because we have to execute the *yoga* system with this material body. In other words, we have to make the best use of a bad bargain. The material body is a bad bargain in the sense that it is the source of all miseries. The spirit soul does not experience misery, and the normal condition of the living entity is his healthy, spiritual life. Misery and disease occur due to material contamination, disease, infection. So in a sense, material existence is a diseased condition of the soul. And what is that disease? The answer is not a great mystery. The disease is this body. This body is actually not meant for me. It may be "my" body, but it is a symptom of my diseased condition. In any case, I should identify with this body no more than I should identify with my clothes. In this world, we are all differently dressed. We are dressed as red men, brown men, white men, black men, yellow men, or as Indians, Americans, Hindus, Muslims, Christians. All these designations are not symptomatic of our actual position but of our diseased condition. The *yoga* system is meant to cure this disease by connecting us again with the Supreme.

We are meant to be connected with the Supreme just as our hand is meant to be connected to our body. We are part and parcel of the Supreme, just as the hand is part and parcel of the body. When the hand is severed from the body, it is valueless, but when it is joined to the body, it is invaluable. Similarly, in this material condition, we are disconnected from God. Actually, the word *disconnected* is not precise, because the connection is always there. God is always supplying all our necessities. Since nothing can exist without Kṛṣṇa, we cannot be disconnected from Him. Rather, it is better to say that we have forgotten that we are connected to Kṛṣṇa. Because of this forgetfulness, we have entered the criminal department of the universe. The government still takes care of its criminals, but they are legally disconnected from the civilian state. Our disconnection is a result of our engaging in so many nonsensical activities instead of utilising our senses in the performance of our Kṛṣṇa conscious duties.

Instead of thinking, "I am the eternal servant of God, or Kṛṣṇa," we are thinking, "I am the servant of my society, my country, my husband, my wife, my dog, or whatever." This is called forgetfulness. How has this come about? All these misconceptions have arisen due to this body. Because I was born in Britain, I am thinking that I am British. Each society teaches its citizens to think in this way. Because I am thinking that I am British, the British government can tell me, "Come and fight. Give your life for your country." This is all due to the bodily conception; therefore an intelligent person should know that he is suffering miseries due to his body and that he should not act in such a way that he will continue to be imprisoned within a material body birth after birth. According to *Padma Purāṇa,* there are 8,400,000 species of life, and all are but different forms of contamination — whether one has a British body, an Indian body, a dog's body, a hog's body or whatever. Therefore the first instruction in *yoga* is, "I am not this body".

Attaining liberation from the contamination of the material body is the first teaching of *Bhagavad-gītā.* In the Second Chapter, after Arjuna told Śrī Kṛṣṇa, "I shall not fight," the Lord said, "While speaking learned words, you are mourning for what is not worthy of grief. Those who are wise lament neither for the living nor the dead." (Bg. 2.11) In other words, Arjuna was thinking on the bodily platform. He wanted to leave the battlefield because he did not want to fight with his relatives. All his conceptions were within the bodily atmosphere; therefore after Arjuna accepted Śrī Kṛṣṇa as his spiritual master, the Lord immediately chastised him, just as a master chastises his disciple in order to teach him. Essentially, Śrī Kṛṣṇa told Arjuna, "You are talking very wisely, as if you know so many things, but actually you are speaking nonsense, because you are speaking from the bodily position." Similarly, people throughout the world are posing themselves as highly advanced in education, science, philosophy, politics, etc., but their position is on the bodily platform.

A vulture may rise very high in the sky — seven or eight miles — and it is wonderful to see him fly in this way. He also has powerful eyes, for he can spot a carcass from a great distance. Yet what is the object of all these great qualifications? A dead body, a rotting carcass. His perfection is just to discover a dead piece of meat and eat it. That's all. Similarly, we may have a very high education, but what is our objective? Sense enjoyment, the enjoyment of this material body. We may rise very high with our spaceships, but what is the purpose? Sense gratification, that's all. This means that all the striving and all this high education are merely on the animal platform.

Therefore we should first of all know that our miserable material condition is due to this body. At the same time, we should know that this body is not permanent. Although I identify with my body, family, society, country and so many other things, how long will these objects exist? They are not permanent. *Asat* is a word meaning that they will cease to exist. *Asann api kleśada āsa dehaḥ:* "The body is simply troublesome and impermanent."

Many people come to us saying, "Svāmījī, my position is so troublesome," but as soon as we suggest the medicine, they will not accept it. This means that people want to manufacture their own medicine. Why do we go to a physician if we want to treat ourselves? People want to accept only what they think is palatable.

Although we are suggesting that this body is useless and is a form of contamination, we are not recommending that it be abused. We may use a car to carry us to work, but this does not mean that we should not take care of the car. We should take care of the car for it to carry us to and fro, but we should not become so attached to it that we are polishing it every day. We must utilise this material body in order to execute Kṛṣṇa consciousness, and to this end we should keep it fit and healthy, but we should not become too attached to it. That is called *yukta-vairāgya.* The body should not be neglected. We should bathe regularly, eat regularly, sleep regularly in order to keep mind and body healthy. Some people say that the body should be renounced and that we should take some drugs and abandon ourselves to intoxication, but this is not a *yoga* process. Kṛṣṇa has given us nice food — fruits, grains, vegetables and milk — and we can prepare hundreds and thousands of nice preparations and offer them to the Lord. Our process is to eat *kṛṣṇa-prasādam* and to satisfy the tongue in that way. But we should not be greedy and eat dozens of *samosās,* sweetballs and *rasagullās.* No. We should eat and sleep just enough to keep the body fit, and no more. It is stated,

yuktāhāra-vihārasya
yukta-ceṣṭasya karmasu
yukta-svapnāvabodhasya
yogo bhavati duḥkha-hā

"He who is regulated in his habits of eating, sleeping, recreation and work can mitigate all material pains by practising the *yoga* system." (Bg. 6.17)

Although we should minimise our eating and sleeping, we should not attempt this too rapidly, at the risk of becoming sick. Because people are accustomed to eating voraciously, there are prescriptions for fasting. We can reduce our sleeping and eating, but we should remain in good health for spiritual purposes. We should not attempt to reduce eating and sleeping too rapidly or artificially; when we advance we will naturally not feel pain due to the reduction of these natural bodily processes. In this respect, Raghunātha dāsa Gosvāmī offers a good example. Although a very rich man's son, Raghunātha dāsa left his home to join Lord Caitanya Mahāprabhu. Because he was the only son, Raghunātha dāsa was very beloved by his father. Understanding that his son had gone to Jagannātha Purī to join Lord Caitanya, the father sent four servants with money to attend him. At first, Raghunātha accepted the money, thinking, "Oh, since my father has sent all this money, I will accept it and invite all the *sannyāsīs* to feast."

After some time, however, the feasts came to an end. Lord Caitanya Mahāprabhu then enquired from His secretary, Svarūpa Dāmodara, "Nowadays I don't receive any invitations from Raghunātha. What has happened?"

"That is because Raghunātha has stopped accepting his father's money."

"Oh, that's very nice," Caitanya Mahāprabhu said.

"Raghunātha was thinking, 'Although I have renounced everything, I am still enjoying my father's money. This is hypocritical.' Therefore he has told the servants to go home and has refused the money."

"So how is he living?" Caitanya Mahāprabhu enquired.

"Oh, he's standing on the steps of the Jagannātha temple, and when the priests pass him on their way home, they offer him some *prasādam.* In this way, he is satisfied."

"This is very nice," Caitanya Mahāprabhu commented.

Regularly going to the Jagannātha temple, Lord Caitanya Mahāprabhu would see Raghunātha standing on the steps. After a few days, however, He no longer saw him there. Therefore the Lord commented to His secretary, "I no longer see Raghunātha standing on the temple steps."

"He has given that up," Svarūpa Dāmodara explained. "He was thinking, 'Oh, I am standing here just like a prostitute, waiting for someone to come and give me food. No. I don't like this at all.' "

"That is very nice," Caitanya Mahāprabhu said, "but how is he eating?"

"Every day he is collecting some rejected rice from the kitchen and is eating that."

To encourage Raghunātha, Caitanya Mahāprabhu one day visited him. "Raghunātha," the Lord said, "I hear that you are eating very palatable food. Why are you not inviting Me?"

Raghunātha did not reply, but the Lord quickly found the place where he kept the rice, and the Lord immediately took some and began to eat it.

"Dear Lord," Raghunātha implored, "please do not eat this. It is not fit for You."

"Oh, no? Why do you say it's not fit for Me? It's Lord Jagannātha's *prasādam*!"

Lord Caitanya Mahāprabhu enacted this pastime just to discourage Raghunātha from thinking, "I am eating this miserable, rejected rice." Through the Lord's encouragement, Raghunātha dāsa Gosvāmī reduced his daily quantity of food until he was finally eating only one pat of butter every other day. And every day he was also bowing down hundreds of times and constantly chanting the holy names. *Saṅkhyā-pūrvaka-nāma-gāna-natibhiḥ kālāvasānī-kṛtau.*

Although this is an excellent example of minimising all material necessities, we should not try to imitate it. It is not possible for an ordinary man to imitate Raghunātha dāsa Gosvāmī, who was one of the six Gosvāmīs, a highly elevated associate of Lord Caitanya Mahāprabhu Himself. Each one of the six Gosvāmīs displayed a unique example of how one can advance in Kṛṣṇa consciousness, but it is not our duty to imitate them. We should just try to follow, as far as possible, in their footsteps. If we immediately try to become like Raghunātha dāsa Gosvāmī by imitating him, we are sure to fail, and whatever progress we have made will be defeated. Therefore the Lord says (Bg. 6.16) that there is no possibility of one's becoming a *yogī* if one eats too much or too little.

The same moderation applies to sleep. Presently I may be sleeping ten hours a day, but if I can keep myself fit by sleeping five hours, why sleep ten? As far as the body is concerned, there are four demands — eating, sleeping, mating and defending. The problem with modern civilisation is that it is trying to increase these demands, but they should be decreased instead. Eat what we need, and sleep when we need, and our health will be excellent. There is no question of artificial imitation.

And what is the result obtained by one who is temperate in his habits?

yadā viniyataṁ cittam
ātmany evāvatiṣṭhate
nispṛhaḥ sarva-kāmebhyo
yukta ity ucyate tadā

"When the *yogī,* by practice of *yoga,* disciplines his mental activities and becomes situated in transcendence — devoid of all material desires — he is said to be well established in *yoga.*" (Bg. 6.18)

The perfection of *yoga* means keeping the mind in a state of equilibrium. Materially speaking, this is impossible. After reading a mundane novel once, you will not want to read it again, but you can read *Bhagavad-gītā* four times a day and still not tire of it. You may chant someone's name a half an hour, or sing a mundane song three or four times, but before long this becomes tiresome. Hare Kṛṣṇa, however, can be chanted day and night, and one will never tire of it.

Therefore it is only through transcendental vibration that the mind can be kept in a state of equilibrium. When one's mental activities are thus stabilised, one is said to have attained *yoga*.

The perfectional stage of *yoga* was exhibited by King Ambarīṣa, who utilised all his senses in the service of the Lord. As stated in *Śrīmad-Bhāgavatam* (9.4.18-20),

sa vai manaḥ kṛṣṇa-padāravindayor
vacāṁsi vaikuṇṭha-guṇānuvarṇane
karau harer mandira-mārjanādiṣu
śrutiṁ cakārācyuta-sat-kathodaye

mukunda-liṅgālaya-darśane dṛśau
tad-bhṛtya-gātra-sparśe 'ṅga-saṅgamam
ghrāṇaṁ ca tat-pāda-saroja-saurabhe
śrīmat-tulasyā rasanaṁ tad-arpite

pādau hareḥ kṣetra-padānusarpaṇe
śiro hṛṣīkeśa-padābhivandane
kāmaṁ ca dāsye na tu kāma-kāmyayā
yathottamaśloka-janāśrayā ratiḥ

"King Ambarīṣa first of all engaged his mind on the lotus feet of Lord Kṛṣṇa; then, one after another, he engaged his words in describing the transcendental qualities of the Lord, his hands in mopping the temple of the Lord, his ears in hearing of the activities of the Lord, his eyes in seeing the transcendental forms of the Lord, his body in touching the bodies of the devotees, his sense of smell in smelling the scents of the lotus flowers offered to the Lord, his tongue in tasting the *tulasī* leaf offered at the temple of the Lord, his head in offering obeisances unto the Lord, and his desires in executing the mission of the Lord. All these transcendental activities are quite befitting a pure devotee."

This, then, is the perfection of *yoga* devoid of all material desire. If all our desires are for Kṛṣṇa, there is no scope for material desire. All material desire is automatically finished. We don't have to try to concentrate artificially. All perfection is there in Kṛṣṇa consciousness because it is on the spiritual platform. Being on the spiritual platform, this supreme *yoga* is eternal, blissful, and full of knowledge. Therefore there are no misgivings or material impediments.

CHAPTER FIVE

Determination and Steadiness in Yoga

yathā dīpo nivāta-stho
neṅgate sopamā smṛtā
yogino yata-cittasya
yuñjato yogam ātmanaḥ

"As a lamp in a windless place does not waver, so the transcendentalist, whose mind is controlled, remains always steady in his meditation on the transcendent self." (Bg. 6.19)

If the mind is absorbed in Kṛṣṇa consciousness, it will remain as steady as the flame of a candle that is in a room where there is no wind. Therefore it is said that a truly Kṛṣṇa conscious person always absorbed in transcendence, in constant undisturbed meditation on his worshipable Lord, is as steady as a lamp or candle in a windless place. Just as the flame is not agitated, the mind is not agitated, and that steadiness is the perfection of *yoga.*

The state of one thus steadily situated in meditation on the transcendent Self, or the Supreme Lord, is described by Śrī Kṛṣṇa in the following verses of *Bhagavad-gītā* (6.20-23):

yatroparamate cittaṁ
niruddhaṁ yoga-sevayā
yatra caivātmanātmānaṁ
paśyann ātmani tuṣyati

sukham ātyantikaṁ yat tad
buddhi-grāhyam atīndriyam

vetti yatra na caivāyaṁ
sthitaś calati tattvataḥ

yaṁ labdhvā cāparaṁ lābhaṁ
manyate nādhikaṁ tataḥ
yasmin sthito na duḥkhena
guruṇāpi vicālyate
taṁ vidyād duḥkha-saṁyoga-
viyogaṁ yoga-saṁjñitam

"In the stage of perfection called trance, or *samādhi,* one's mind is completely restrained from material mental activities by practise of *yoga.* This perfection is characterised by one's ability to see the self by the pure mind and to relish and rejoice in the self. In that joyous state, one is situated in boundless transcendental happiness, realized through transcendental senses. Established thus, one never departs from the truth, and upon gaining this he thinks there is no greater gain. Being situated in such a position, one is never shaken, even in the midst of greatest difficulty. This indeed is actual freedom from all miseries arising from material contact."

Samādhi does not mean making oneself void or merging into the void. That is impossible. *Kleśo 'dhikataras teṣām avyaktāsakta-cetasām.* Some *yogīs* say that one has to put an end to all activities and make himself motionless, but how is this possible? By nature, the living entity is a moving, acting spirit. "Motionless" means putting an end to material motion and being fixed in Kṛṣṇa consciousness. In such a state, one is no longer disturbed by material propensities. As one becomes materially motionless, one's motions in Kṛṣṇa consciousness increase. As one becomes active in Kṛṣṇa consciousness, one becomes automatically motionless in respect to material activities.

I have often used the example of a restless child. Since it is impossible to make such a child motionless, it is necessary to give him some playthings or some pictures to look at. In this way, he will be engaged, or motionless in the sense that he will not be committing some mischief. But if one really wants to make him motionless, one must give him some engagement in Kṛṣṇa consciousness. Then there will be no scope for mischievous activities, due to realisation in Kṛṣṇa consciousness. To be engaged in Kṛṣṇa consciousness, one should first realise, "I am Kṛṣṇa's. I am not this matter. I am not of this nation or of this society. I do not belong to this rascal or that rascal. I am simply Kṛṣṇa's." This is motionless; this is full knowledge, realising our actual position as part and parcel of Kṛṣṇa. As stated in the Fifteenth Chapter (Bg. 15.7), *mamaivāṁśo jīva-loke:* "The living entities in this conditioned world are My eternal fragmental parts." As soon as we understand this, we immediately cease our material activities, and this is what is meant by being motionless. In this state, one sees the Self by the pure mind and relishes and rejoices in the Self. "Pure mind" means understanding, "I belong to Kṛṣṇa." At the present moment, the mind is contaminated because we are thinking, "I belong to this; I belong to that." The mind is pure when it understands, "I belong to Kṛṣṇa."

Rejoicing in the Self means rejoicing with Kṛṣṇa. Kṛṣṇa is the Supersoul, or the Superself. I am the individual soul, or the individual self. The Superself and the self enjoy together. Enjoyment cannot be alone; there must be two. What experience do we have of solitary enjoyment? Solitary enjoyment is not possible. Enjoyment means two: Kṛṣṇa, who is the Supersoul, and the individual soul.

If one is convinced that "I am part and parcel of Kṛṣṇa," one is not disturbed even in the midst of the greatest difficulties, because one knows that Kṛṣṇa will give protection. That is surrender. To attain this position, one must try his best, use his intelligence, and believe in Kṛṣṇa. *Bālasya neha śaraṇaṁ pitarau nṛsiṁha* (*Bhāg.* 7.9.19). If Kṛṣṇa does not protect us, nothing can save us. If Kṛṣṇa neglects us, there is no remedy, and whatever measures we take to try to protect ourselves will be ultimately defeated. There may be many expert physicians treating a diseased man, but that is no guarantee that he will live. If Kṛṣṇa so wills, a person will die despite the best physicians and medicines. On the other hand, if Kṛṣṇa is protecting us, we will survive even without medical treatment. When one is fully surrendered to Kṛṣṇa, he becomes happy, knowing that regardless of the situation, Kṛṣṇa will protect him. He is just like a child who is fully surrendered to his parents, confident that they are there to protect him. As stated by Yāmunācārya in his *Stotra-ratna* (43), *kadāham aikāntika-nitya-kiṅkaraḥ praharṣayiṣyāmi sanātha-jīvitam:* "O Lord, when shall I engage as Your permanent, eternal servant and always feel joyful to have such a perfect master?" If we know that there is someone very powerful who is our patron and saviour, aren't we happy? But if we try to act on our own and at our own risk, how can we be happy? Happiness means being in Kṛṣṇa consciousness and being convinced that "Kṛṣṇa will give me protection," and being true to Kṛṣṇa. It is not possible to be happy otherwise.

Of course, Kṛṣṇa is giving all living entities protection, even in their rebellious condition (*eko bahūnāṁ yo vidadhāti kāmān*). Without Kṛṣṇa's protection, we cannot live for a second. When we admit and recognise Kṛṣṇa's kindness, we become happy. Kṛṣṇa is protecting us at every moment, but we do not realise this, because we have taken life at our own risk. Kṛṣṇa gives us a certain amount of freedom, saying, "All right, do whatever you like. As far as possible, I will give you protection." However, when the living entity is fully surrendered to Kṛṣṇa, Kṛṣṇa takes total charge and gives special protection. If a child grows up and doesn't care for his father and acts freely, what can his father do? He can only say, "Do whatever you like." But when a son puts himself fully under his father's protection, he receives more care. As Kṛṣṇa states in the Ninth Chapter of *Bhagavad-gītā* (9.29),

samo 'haṁ sarva-bhūteṣu
na me dveṣyo 'sti na priyaḥ
ye bhajanti tu māṁ bhaktyā
mayi te teṣu cāpy aham

"I envy no one, nor am I partial to anyone. I am equal to all. But whoever renders service unto Me in devotion is a friend, is in Me, and I am also a friend to him."

How can Kṛṣṇa be envious of anyone? Everyone is Kṛṣṇa's son. Similarly, how can Kṛṣṇa be an enemy toward anyone? Since all living entities are Kṛṣṇa's sons, He is everyone's friend. Unfortunately, we are not taking advantage of His friendship, and that is our disease. Once we recognise Kṛṣṇa as our eternal father and friend, we can understand that He is always protecting us, and in this way we can be happy.

sa niścayena yoktavyo
yogo 'nirviṇṇa-cetasā
saṅkalpa-prabhavān kāmāṁs
tyaktvā sarvān aśeṣataḥ
manasaivendriya-grāmaṁ
viniyamya samantataḥ

"One should engage oneself in the practice of *yoga* with determination and faith. One should abandon, without exception, all material desires born of mental speculation and thus control all the senses on all sides by the mind." (Bg. 6.24)

As stated before, this determination can be attained only by one who does not indulge in sex. Celibacy makes one's determination strong; therefore, from the very beginning Kṛṣṇa states that the *yogī* does not engage in sex. If one indulges in sex, one's determination will be flickering. Therefore sex life should be controlled according to the rules and regulations governing the *gṛhastha-āśrama,* or sex should be given up altogether. Actually, it should be given up altogether, but if this is not possible, it should be controlled. Then determination will come because, after all, determination is a bodily affair. Determination means continuing to practise Kṛṣṇa consciousness with patience and perseverance. If one does not immediately attain the desired results, one should not think, "Oh, what is this Kṛṣṇa consciousness? I will give it up." No, we must have determination and faith in Kṛṣṇa's words.

In this regard, there is a mundane example. When a young girl gets married, she immediately hankers for a child. She thinks, "Now I am married. I must have a child immediately." But how is this possible? The girl must have patience, become a faithful wife, serve her husband, and let her love grow. Eventually, because she is married, it is certain that she will have a child. Similarly, when we are in Kṛṣṇa consciousness, our perfection is guaranteed, but we must have patience and determination. We should think, "I must execute my duties and should not be impatient." Impatience is due to loss of determination, and loss of determination is due to excessive sex.

The *yogī* should be determined and should patiently prosecute Kṛṣṇa consciousness without deviation. One should be sure of success at the end and pursue this course with great perseverance, not becoming discouraged if there is any delay in the attainment of success. Success is sure for the rigid practitioner. Regarding *bhakti-yoga,* Rūpa Gosvāmī says,

utsāhān niścayād dhairyāt
tat-tat-karma-pravartanāt
saṅga-tyāgāt sato vṛtteḥ
ṣaḍbhir bhaktiḥ prasidhyati

"The process of *bhakti-yoga* can be executed successfully with full-hearted enthusiasm, perseverance and determination by following the prescribed duties in the association of devotees and by engaging completely in activities of goodness." (*Upadeśāmṛta* 3)

As for determination, one should follow the example of the sparrow who lost her eggs in the waves of the ocean. A sparrow laid her eggs on the shore of the ocean, but the big ocean carried away the eggs on its waves. The sparrow became very upset and asked the ocean to return her eggs. The ocean did not even consider her appeal. So the sparrow decided to dry up the ocean. She began to pick out the water in her small beak, and everyone laughed at her for her impossible determination. The news of her activity spread, and when at last Garuḍa, the gigantic bird carrier of Lord Viṣṇu, heard it, he became compassionate toward his small sister bird, and so he came to see her. Garuḍa was very pleased by the determination of the small sparrow, and he promised to help. Thus Garuḍa at once asked the ocean to return her eggs lest he himself take up the work of the sparrow. The ocean was frightened by this, and returned the eggs. Thus the sparrow became happy by the grace of Garuḍa.

Similarly, the practise of *yoga,* especially *bhakti-yoga* in Kṛṣṇa consciousness, may appear to be a very difficult job. But if anyone follows the principles with great determination, the Lord will surely help, for God helps those who help themselves,

śanaiḥ śanair uparamed
buddhyā dhṛti-gṛhītayā
ātma-saṁsthaṁ manaḥ kṛtvā
na kiñcid api cintayet

"Gradually, step by step, one should become situated in trance by means of intelligence sustained by full conviction, and thus the mind should be fixed on the self alone and should think of nothing else." (Bg. 6.25)

We are the self, and Kṛṣṇa is also the Self. When there is sunlight, we can see the sun and ourselves also. However, when there is dense darkness, we sometimes cannot even see our own body. Although the body is there, the darkness is so dense that I cannot see myself. But when the sunshine is present, I can see myself as well as the sun. Similarly, seeing the self means first of all seeing the Supreme Self, Kṛṣṇa. In the *Kaṭha Upaniṣad* it is stated, *nityo nityānāṁ cetanaś cetanānām:* "The Supreme Self is the chief eternal of all eternals, and He is the chief living being of all living beings." Kṛṣṇa consciousness means fixing the mind on Kṛṣṇa, and when the mind is thus fixed, it is fixed on the complete whole. If the stomach is cared for and supplied nutritious food, all the bodily limbs are nourished, and we are in good health. Similarly, if we water the root of a tree, all the branches, leaves, flowers and twigs are automatically taken care of. By rendering service to Kṛṣṇa, we automatically render the best service to all others.

As stated before, a Kṛṣṇa conscious person does not sit down idly. He knows that Kṛṣṇa consciousness is such an important philosophy that it should be distributed. Therefore the members of this Kṛṣṇa consciousness society are not just sitting in the temple but are going out on *saṅkīrtana* parties, preaching and distributing this supreme philosophy. That is the mission of Śrī Kṛṣṇa Caitanya Mahāprabhu and His disciples. Other *yogīs* may be satisfied with their own elevation and sit in secluded places, practising *yoga.* For them, *yoga* is nothing more than their personal concern. A devotee, however, is not satisfied just in elevating his personal self.

vāñchā-kalpatarubhyaś ca
kṛpā-sindhubhya eva ca
patitānāṁ pāvanebhyo
vaiṣṇavebhyo namo namaḥ

"I offer my respectful obeisances unto all the Vaiṣṇava devotees of the Lord, who can fulfil the desires of everyone, just like desire trees, and who are full of compassion for the fallen souls." A devotee displays great compassion toward conditioned souls. The word *kṛpā* means "mercy", and *sindhu* means "ocean". A devotee is an ocean of mercy, and he naturally wants to distribute this mercy. Lord Jesus Christ, for instance, was God conscious, Kṛṣṇa conscious, but he was not satisfied in keeping this knowledge within himself. Had he continued to live alone in God consciousness, he would not have met crucifixion. But no. Being a devotee and naturally compassionate, he also wanted to take care of others by making them God conscious. Although he was forbidden to preach God consciousness, he continued to do so at the risk of his own life. This is the nature of a devotee.

It is therefore stated in *Bhagavad-gītā* (18.68-69) that the devotee who preaches is most dear to the Lord:

ya idaṁ paramaṁ guhyaṁ
mad-bhakteṣv abhidhāsyati

bhaktiṁ mayi parāṁ kṛtvā
mām evaiṣyaty asaṁśayaḥ

"For one who explains this supreme secret to the devotees, pure devotional service is guaranteed, and at the end he will come back to Me."

na ca tasmān manuṣyeṣu
kaścin me priya-kṛttamaḥ
bhavitā na ca me tasmād
anyaḥ priyataro bhuvi

"There is no servant in this world more dear to Me than he, nor will there ever be one more dear." Therefore the devotees go out to preach, and going forth, they sometimes meet opposing elements. Sometimes they are defeated, sometimes disappointed, sometimes able to convince, sometimes unable. It is not that every devotee is well equipped to preach. Just as there are different types of people, there are three classes of devotees. In the third class are those who have no faith. If they are engaged in devotional service officially, for some ulterior purpose, they cannot achieve the highest perfectional stage. Most probably they will slip, after some time. They may become engaged, but because they haven't complete conviction and faith, it is very difficult for them to continue in Kṛṣṇa consciousness. We have practical experience in discharging our missionary activity that some people come and apply themselves to Kṛṣṇa consciousness with some hidden motive, and as soon as they are economically a little well situated, they give up this process and take to their old ways again. It is only by faith that one can advance in Kṛṣṇa consciousness. As far as the development of faith is concerned, one who is well versed in the literatures of devotional service and has attained the stage of firm faith is called a first-class person in Kṛṣṇa consciousness. And in the second class are those who are not very advanced in understanding the devotional scriptures but who automatically have firm faith that *kṛṣṇa-bhakti,* or service to Kṛṣṇa, is the best course and so in good faith have taken it up. Thus they are superior to the third class, who have neither perfect knowledge of the scriptures nor good faith but by association and simplicity are trying to follow. The third-class person in Kṛṣṇa consciousness may fall down, but when one is in the second class or first class, he does not fall down. One in the first class will surely make progress and achieve the result at the end. As far as the third-class person in Kṛṣṇa consciousness is concerned, although he has faith in the conviction that devotional service to Kṛṣṇa is very good, he has no knowledge of Kṛṣṇa through the scriptures like the *Śrīmad-Bhāgavatam* and *Bhagavad-gītā.* Sometimes these third-class persons in Kṛṣṇa consciousness have a tendency toward *karma-yoga* and *jñāna-yoga,* and sometimes they are disturbed, but as soon as the infection of *karma-yoga* or *jñāna-yoga* is vanquished, they become second-class or first-class persons in Kṛṣṇa consciousness. Faith in Kṛṣṇa is also divided into three stages and described in *Śrīmad-Bhāgavatam.* First-class attachment, second-class attachment and third-class attachment are also explained in *Śrīmad-Bhāgavatam,* in the Eleventh Canto.

However one is situated, one should have the determination to go out and preach Kṛṣṇa consciousness. That endeavour should at least be there, and one who so attempts to preach renders the best service to the Lord. Despite opposition, one should attempt to elevate people to the highest standard of self-realisation. One who has actually seen the truth, who is in the trance of self-realisation, cannot just sit idly. He must come out. Rāmānujācārya, for instance, declared the Hare Kṛṣṇa *mantra* publicly. He did not distribute it secretly for some fee. Recently, an Indian *yogī* came to

England to give some "private *mantra*". But if a mantra has any power, why should it be private? If a *mantra* is powerful, why should it not be publicly declared so that everyone can take advantage of it? We are saying that this Hare Kṛṣṇa *mahā-mantra* can save everyone, and we are therefore distributing it publicly, free of charge. But in this age, people are so foolish that they are not prepared to accept it. Rather, they hanker after some secret *mantra* and therefore pay some "*yogī*" thirty-five pounds or whatever for some "private *mantra*". This is because people want to be cheated. But the devotees are preaching without charge, declaring in the streets, parks and everywhere, "Here! Here is the Hare Kṛṣṇa *mahā-mantra.* Come on, take it!" But under the spell of *māyā,* illusion, people are thinking, "Oh, this is not good." But if you charge something and bluff and cheat people, they will follow you.

In this regard, there is a Hindi verse stating that Kali-yuga is such an abominable age that if one speaks the truth, people will come and beat him. But if one cheats, bluffs and lies, people will be bewildered, will like it and will accept it. If I say, "I am God," people will say, "Oh, here is Svāmījī. Here is God." In this age, people don't have sufficient brain power to enquire, "How have you become God? What are the symptoms of God? Do you have all these symptoms?" Because people do not make such enquiries, they are cheated. Therefore it is necessary to be fixed in consciousness of the Self. Unless one knows and understands the real self and the Superself, one will be cheated. Real *yoga* means understanding this process of self-realisation.

yato yato niścalati
manaś cañcalam asthiram
tatas tato niyamyaitad
ātmany eva vaśaṁ nayet

"From wherever the mind wanders due to its flickering and unsteady nature, one must certainly withdraw it and bring it back under the control of the self." (Bg. 6.26) This is the real yogic process. If you are trying to concentrate your mind on Kṛṣṇa, and the mind is diverted — wandering to some cinema or wherever — you should withdraw the mind, thinking, "Not there, please. Here." This is *yoga*: not allowing the mind to wander from Kṛṣṇa.

Very intense training is required to keep the mind fixed on Kṛṣṇa while sitting in one place. That is very hard work indeed. If one is not so practised and tries to imitate this process, he will surely be confused. Instead, we always have to engage ourselves in Kṛṣṇa consciousness, dovetailing everything we do to Kṛṣṇa. Our usual activities should be so moulded that they are rendered for Kṛṣṇa's sake. In this way the mind will remain fixed on Kṛṣṇa. As stated before, we should not try to sit down and stare at the tip of our nose. At the present moment, attempts to engage in that type of *yoga* are artificial. Rather, the recommended method is chanting loudly and hearing Hare Kṛṣṇa. Then, even if the mind is diverted, it will be forced to concentrate on the sound vibration "Kṛṣṇa". It isn't necessary to withdraw the mind from everything; it will automatically be withdrawn, because it will be concentrated on the sound vibration. If we hear an automobile pass, our attention is automatically diverted. Similarly, if we constantly chant Hare Kṛṣṇa, our mind will automatically be fixed on Kṛṣṇa, although we are accustomed to think of so many other things.

The nature of the mind is flickering and unsteady. But a self-realised *yogī* has to control the mind; the mind should not control him. At the present moment, the mind is controlling us (*go-dāsa*). The mind is telling us, "Please, why not look at that beautiful girl?" and so we look. It says,

"Why not drink that nice liquor?" and we say, "Yes." It says, "Why not smoke this cigarette?" "Yes," we say. "Why not go to this restaurant for such palatable food? Why not do this? Why not do that?" In this way, the mind is dictating, and we are following. Material life means being controlled by the senses, or the mind, which is the centre of all the senses. Being controlled by the mind means being controlled by the senses, because the senses are the mind's assistants. The master mind dictates, "Go see that," and the eyes, following the directions of the mind, look at the sense object. The mind tells us to go to a certain place, and the legs, under the mind's directions, carry us there. Thus, being under the direction of the mind means coming under the control of the senses. If we can control the mind, we will not be under the control of the senses. One who is under the control of the senses is known as *go-dāsa*. The word *go* means "senses", and *dāsa* means "servant". One who is master of the senses is called *gosvāmī,* because *svāmī* means "master". Therefore, one who has the title *gosvāmī* is one who has mastered the senses. As long as one is servant of the senses, he cannot be called a *gosvāmī* or *svāmī*. Unless one masters the senses, his acceptance of the title *svāmī* or *gosvāmī* is just a form of cheating. It was Rūpa Gosvāmī who thus defined the meaning of the word *gosvāmī*. Originally, Sanātana Gosvāmī and Rūpa Gosvāmī were not *gosvāmīs* but were government ministers. It was only when they became disciples of Lord Caitanya Mahāprabhu that they became *gosvāmīs*. So *gosvāmī* is not a hereditary title but a qualification. One becomes so qualified under the directions of a bona fide spiritual master. Only when one has attained perfection in sense control can he be called a *gosvāmī* and become a spiritual master in his turn. Unless one can master the senses, he will simply be a bogus spiritual master.

This is explained by Śrīla Rūpa Gosvāmī in his *Upadeś-āmṛta* (1):

vāco vegaṁ manasaḥ krodha-vegaṁ
jihvā-vegam udaropastha-vegam
etān vegān yo viṣaheta dhīraḥ
sarvām apīmāṁ pṛthivīṁ sa śiṣyāt

"A sober person who can tolerate the urge to speak, the mind's demands, the actions of anger, and the urges of the tongue, belly and genitals is qualified to make disciples all over the world." In this verse Rūpa Gosvāmī mentions six "pushings" (*vegam*). This pushing is a kind of impetus. For instance, when nature calls, we have to go to the toilet, and we cannot check this urge. So this urge is called *vegam,* a kind of pushing. According to Rūpa Gosvāmī, there are six *vegams. Vāco vegam* is the urge to talk unnecessarily. That is a kind of pushing of the tongue. Then there is *krodha-vegam,* the urge to become angry. When we are pushed to anger, we cannot check ourselves, and sometimes men become so angry that they commit murder. Similarly, the mind is pushing, dictating, "You must go there at once," and we immediately go where we are told. The word *jihvā-vegam* refers to the tongue's being urged to taste palatable foods. *Udara-vegam* refers to the urges of the belly. Although the belly is full, it still wants more food, and that is a kind of pushing of the belly. And when we yield to the pushings of the tongue and the belly, the urges of the genitals become very strong, and sex is required. If one does not control his mind or his tongue, how can he control his genitals? In this way, there are so many pushings, so much so that the body is a kind of pushing machine. Rūpa Gosvāmī therefore tells us that one can become a spiritual master only when he can control all these urges.

Etān vegān yo viṣaheta dhīraḥ sarvām apīmāṁ pṛthivīm sa śiṣyāt: "One who can control the pushings and remain steady can make disciples all over the world." The word *dhīra* means "steady, sober". Only one who is a *dhīra* is qualified to make disciples. This all depends on one's training. Indeed, *yoga* means training the mind and the senses to be fixed on the Self. This is not possible by meditating only fifteen minutes a day and then going out and doing whatever the senses dictate. How can the problems of life be solved so cheaply? If we want something precious, we have to pay for it. By the grace of Lord Caitanya, this payment has been made very easy—just chant Hare Kṛṣṇa. By our chanting, this system of control, this *yoga* system, becomes perfected. *Ihā haite sarva siddhi haibe tomāra.* Thus Lord Caitanya has blessed us. Simply by chanting Hare Kṛṣṇa, we will achieve the perfection of self-realisation. In this age of Kali-yuga, when people are so fallen, other processes will not be successful. This is the only process, and it is easy, sublime, effective and practical. By it, one can realise oneself.

According to Kṛṣṇa in the Ninth Chapter of *Bhagavad-gītā* (9.2), this process is the most sublime.

rāja-vidyā rāja-guhyaṁ
pavitram idam uttamam
pratyakṣāvagamaṁ dharmyaṁ
su-sukhaṁ kartum avyayam

"This knowledge is the king of education, the most secret of all secrets. It is the purest knowledge, and because it gives direct perception of the self by realisation, it is the perfection of religion. It is everlasting, and it is joyfully performed."

After eating, a man can understand that his hunger has been satisfied; similarly, by following the principles of Kṛṣṇa consciousness, one can understand that he has advanced in self-realisation.

CHAPTER SIX

Perception of the Supersoul

praśānta-manasaṁ hy enaṁ
yoginaṁ sukham uttamam
upaiti śānta-rajasaṁ
brahma-bhūtam akalmaṣam

"The *yogī* whose mind is fixed on Me verily attains the highest perfection of transcendental happiness. He is beyond the mode of passion, he realizes his qualitative identity with the Supreme, and thus he is freed from all reactions to past deeds." (Bg. 6.27)

yuñjann evaṁ sadātmānaṁ
yogī vigata-kalmaṣaḥ
sukhena brahma-saṁsparśam
atyantaṁ sukham aśnute

"Thus the self-controlled *yogī*, constantly engaged in *yoga* practice, becomes free from all material contamination and achieves the highest stage of perfect happiness in transcendental loving service to the Lord." (Bg. 6.28)

So here is the perfection: "The *yogī* whose mind is fixed on Me." Since Kṛṣṇa is speaking, the "Me" refers to Kṛṣṇa. If I am speaking and saying, "Give me a glass of water," I do not intend that the water be supplied to someone else. We must therefore clearly understand that, since *Bhagavad-*

His Divine Grace
A. C. Bhaktivedanta Swami Prabhupāda
Founder-*Ācārya* of the International Society for Krishna Consciousness

"When Caitanya Mahāprabhu appeared five hundred years ago in India, He was always dancing and chanting Hare Kṛṣṇa. In Kṛṣṇa consciousness, our recreation is dancing and chanting, and when we get tired we take *prasāda,* spiritual food. Is dancing difficult? Is chanting difficult? It is natural to enjoy music and dancing and palatable vegetarian foods. These are our recreations, and this is our method of meditation." (*p. 10*)

Pleasure is the ultimate goal of *yoga.* This pleasure is not a solitary affair; rather, it is experienced as part of the soul's eternal spiritual relationship with the Supreme Soul, Kṛṣṇa. The *yogī* seeking to attain this perfectional stage therefore meditates upon Kṛṣṇa's associates in the spiritual world, the chief of whom is Rādhā. (*p. 11*)

"A *yogī* who is practising meditation on the Supersoul sees within himself the plenary portion of Kṛṣṇa as Viṣṇu—with four hands, holding conchshell, wheel, club, and lotus flower." (*pp. 94-95*)

"The *yogī* finds out where Lord Viṣṇu is seated within his heart, and when he finds this form there, he concentrates on Him. The *yogī* should know that this Viṣṇu is not different from Kṛṣṇa. Kṛṣṇa in this form of Supersoul is situated in everyone's heart." (*p. 97*)

"Purification of consciousness is the purpose of the *yoga* system. At death, the finer elements of our bodies (mind, intelligence and ego), which, combined, are called consciousness, carry the small particle of spirit soul to another body to suffer or enjoy, according to one's work." (*pp. 112-113*)

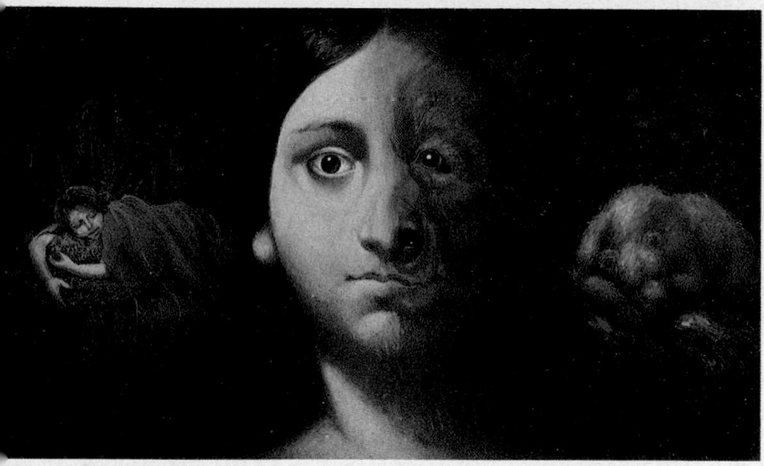

One's thoughts and actions in one's present life determine
he type of body one will receive in one's next life. If one likes
o eat meat. one may get the body of a tiger. One who is
gluttonous may get the body of a pig. If one takes pleasure in
exposing one's body, one may get the body of a tree, which
must stand in all types of weather. Or if one likes to sleep,
one may get the body of a bear.

The *yogī* would hold postures and meditate not for fifteen minutes or half an hour but for years on end. He would discipline himself to endure all the physical discomforts caused by the weather, and even when approached by a tiger, he would remain fearless. Finally, he had to raise his soul on his life airs to the top of his skull and cause the soul to leave the body at an astrologically auspicious moment.

gītā is being spoken by Śrī Kṛṣṇa, when He says "unto Me", He means unto Kṛṣṇa. Unfortunately, there are many commentators who deviate from these clear instructions. I do not know why; their motives are no doubt nefarious.

sarva-bhūta-stham ātmānaṁ
sarva-bhūtāni cātmani
īkṣate yoga-yuktātmā
sarvatra sama-darśanaḥ

"A true *yogī* observes Me in all beings, and also sees every being in Me. Indeed, the self-realised person sees Me, the same Supreme Lord, everywhere." (Bg. 6.29) *Sarva-bhūta-stham ātmānam:* "A true *yogī* observes Me in all beings." How is this possible? Some people say that all beings are Kṛṣṇa and that therefore there is no point in worshipping Kṛṣṇa separately. Consequently, such people take to humanitarian activities, claiming that such work is better. They say, "Why should Kṛṣṇa be worshipped? Kṛṣṇa says that one should see Kṛṣṇa in every being. Therefore let us serve *daridra-nārāyaṇa,* the man in the street." Such misinterpreters do not know the proper techniques, which have to be learned under a bona fide spiritual master.

A true *yogī,* as explained before, is the devotee of Kṛṣṇa, and the most advanced devotee goes forth to preach Kṛṣṇa consciousness. Why? Because he sees Kṛṣṇa in all beings. How is this? Because he sees that all beings are part and parcel of Kṛṣṇa. He also understands that since these beings have forgotten Kṛṣṇa, it is his duty to awaken them to Kṛṣṇa consciousness. Sometimes missionaries go forth to educate primitive, uneducated people just because they see that they are human beings and so deserve to be educated in order to understand the value of life. This is due to the missionary's sympathy. The devotee is similarly motivated. He understands that everyone should know himself to be part and parcel of Kṛṣṇa. The devotee understands that people are suffering due to their forgetfulness of Kṛṣṇa.

Thus the devotee sees Kṛṣṇa in everything. He is not under the illusion that everything has become Kṛṣṇa. Rather, he sees every living being as the son of God. If I say that this boy is the son of Mr Johnson, do I mean that this boy is Mr Johnson himself? I may see Mr Johnson in this boy because this boy is his son, but the distinction remains. If I see every living being as the son of Kṛṣṇa, I see Kṛṣṇa in every being. This should not be difficult to understand. It is neither an association nor a vision but a fact.

When a devotee sees a cat or a dog, he sees Kṛṣṇa in him. He knows that a cat, for instance, is a living being, and that due to his past deeds he has received the body of a cat. This is due to his forgetfulness. The devotee helps the cat by giving it some *kṛṣṇa-prasādam* so that someday the cat will come to Kṛṣṇa consciousness. This is seeing Kṛṣṇa in the cat. The devotee does not think, "Oh, here is Kṛṣṇa. Let me embrace this cat and serve this cat as God." Such thinking is nonsensical. If one sees a tiger, he does not say, "Oh, here is Kṛṣṇa. Come on, please eat me." The devotee does not embrace all beings as Kṛṣṇa but rather sympathises with every living being because he sees all beings as part and parcel of Kṛṣṇa. In this way, "the true *yogī* observes Me in all beings." This is real vision.

Whatever is done in Kṛṣṇa consciousness, knowingly or unknowingly, will have its effect. Children who bow down or try to vibrate Kṛṣṇa's names or clap during *kīrtana* are actually accumulating so much in their bank account of Kṛṣṇa consciousness. Fire will act, whether one is a child or an adult. If a child touches fire, the fire will burn. The fire does not say, "Oh, I will not burn him. He is a child and does not know." No, the fire will always act as fire. Similarly, Kṛṣṇa is the supreme spirit, and if a child partakes in Kṛṣṇa consciousness, he will be affected. Kṛṣṇa will act, whether the child knows or does not know. Every living being should be given a chance to partake of Kṛṣṇa consciousness because Kṛṣṇa is there and will act. Therefore everyone is being invited to come and take *prasādam*, because this *prasādam* will someday take effect.

We should be careful not to make the mistake of thinking that everyone is Kṛṣṇa; rather, we should see Kṛṣṇa in everyone. Kṛṣṇa is all-pervading. Why is He to be seen only in human beings? As stated in *Brahma-saṁhitā*, He is also present within the atom: *aṇḍāntara-stha-paramāṇu-cayāntara-stham.* The word *paramāṇu* means "atom", and we should understand that Kṛṣṇa is present within every atom. "A true *yogī* observes Me in all beings and also sees every being in Me." How does the *yogī* see every being "in Me"? This is possible because the true *yogī* knows that everything that we see is Kṛṣṇa. We are sitting on this floor or on this carpet, but in actuality we are sitting on Kṛṣṇa. We should know this to be a fact. How is this carpet Kṛṣṇa? It is Kṛṣṇa because it is made of Kṛṣṇa's energy. The Supreme Lord has various energies, of which there are three primary divisions — material energy, spiritual energy and marginal energy. *Parāsya śaktir vividhaiva śrūyate.* We living entities are marginal energy, the material world is material energy and the spiritual world is spiritual energy. We are marginal energy in the sense that we can be either spiritually or materially situated. There is no third alternative; either we become materialistic or spiritualistic.

As long as we are in the material world, we are seated on the material energy, and therefore we are situated in Kṛṣṇa, because Kṛṣṇa's energy is not separate from Kṛṣṇa. A flame contains both heat and illumination, two energies. Neither the heat nor the illumination are separate from the flame; therefore in one sense heat is fire, and illumination is fire, but they can be distinguished. Similarly, this material energy is also Kṛṣṇa, and although we are thinking that we are sitting on this floor, we are actually sitting on Kṛṣṇa. Therefore it is stated, "The self-realised man sees Me everywhere." Seeing Kṛṣṇa everywhere means seeing every living being as well as everything else in relationship to Kṛṣṇa. In the Seventh Chapter of *Bhagavad-gītā* (7.8), Lord Kṛṣṇa tells Arjuna how He can be seen in various manifestations.

raso 'ham apsu kaunteya
prabhāsmi śaśi-sūryayoḥ
praṇavaḥ sarva-vedeṣu
śabdaḥ khe pauruṣaṁ nṛṣu

"O son of Kuntī [Arjuna], I am the taste of water, the light of the sun and the moon, the syllable *oṁ* in the Vedic *mantras;* I am the sound in ether and ability in man."

Water is drunk by all living entities, and is needed by birds, beasts, and man. It is not only used for drinking, but for washing and for cultivating plants as well. A soldier on the battlefield can understand how important water is. When fighting, soldiers become thirsty, and if they have no water, they die. Once a person has learned the philosophy of *Bhagavad-gītā,* whenever he drinks water, he sees Kṛṣṇa. And when does a day pass when we do not drink water? This is the way of Kṛṣṇa consciousness. "I am the light of the sun and the moon." So whether in the day or the night, we see either sunshine or moonshine. How, then, can we forget Kṛṣṇa? This, then, is the way of perfect *yoga.* We have to see Kṛṣṇa everywhere and at all times.

yo māṁ paśyati sarvatra
sarvaṁ ca mayi paśyati

tasyāhaṁ na praṇaśyāmi
sa ca me na praṇaśyati

"For one who sees Me everywhere and sees everything in Me, I am never lost, nor is he ever lost to Me." (Bg. 6.30) This is *sadā tad-bhāva-bhāvitaḥ:* always remembering Kṛṣṇa. If we practise living in this way, we never lose Kṛṣṇa and are never lost to Kṛṣṇa, and at the time of death we are therefore sure to go to Kṛṣṇa. If we are not lost to Kṛṣṇa, where can we go but to Kṛṣṇa? In the Ninth Chapter, Kṛṣṇa tells Arjuna, *kaunteya pratijānīhi na me bhaktaḥ praṇaśyati* (Bg. 9.31): "O son of Kuntī, declare it boldly that My devotee never perishes."

Simply don't lose sight of Kṛṣṇa. That is the perfection of life. We can forget everything else, but we should never forget Kṛṣṇa. If we can remember Kṛṣṇa, we are the richest of men, even though people may see us as very poor. Although Rūpa Gosvāmī and Sanātana Gosvāmī were learned scholars and very opulent ministers, they adopted the poor life of mendicants. In his *Śrī Ṣaḍ-gosvāmy-aṣṭaka* (verse 4), Śrīnivāsa Ācārya thus describes the six Gosvāmīs:

tyaktvā tūrṇam aśeṣa-maṇḍala-pati-śreṇīṁ sadā tucchavat
bhūtvā dīna-gaṇeśakau karuṇayā kaupīna-kanthāśritau
gopī-bhāva-rasāmṛtābdhi-laharī-kallola-magnau muhur
vande rūpa-sanātanau raghu-yugau śrī-jīva-gopālakau

"I offer my respectful obeisances unto the six Gosvāmīs — Śrī Rūpa Gosvāmī, Śrī Sanātana Gosvāmī, Śrī Raghunātha Bhaṭṭa Gosvāmī, Śrī Raghunātha dāsa Gosvāmī, Śrī Jīva Gosvāmī and Śrī Gopāla Bhaṭṭa Gosvāmī — who cast off all aristocratic association as insignificant. To deliver poor, conditioned souls, they accepted loincloths and became mendicants, but they were always merged in the ecstatic ocean of the *gopīs'* love for Kṛṣṇa, and they were always bathing repeatedly in the waves of that ocean."

The words *kaupīna-kanthāśritau* indicate that the Gosvāmīs were simply wearing underwear and a loincloth and nothing else. In other words, they accepted the poorest way of life as mendicants. Generally, if one is habituated to living according to a high standard, he cannot immediately lower his standard. If a rich man accepts such a poor condition, he cannot live, but the Gosvāmīs lived very happily. How was this possible? *Gopī-bhāva-rasāmṛtābdhi-laharī-kallola-magnau muhur/ vande rūpa-sanātanau raghu-yugau śrī-jīva-gopālakau.* They were actually rich because they were constantly dipping themselves in the ocean of the loving affairs of the *gopīs.* If one simply thinks of the *gopīs'* love for Kṛṣṇa, one is not lost. There are many ways not to lose sight of Kṛṣṇa. If we do not lose sight of Kṛṣṇa, then we will not be lost.

A person in Kṛṣṇa consciousness certainly sees Lord Kṛṣṇa everywhere, and he sees everything in Kṛṣṇa. Such a person may appear to see all separate manifestations of the material nature, but in each and every instance he is conscious of Kṛṣṇa, knowing that everything is the manifestation of Kṛṣṇa's energy. Nothing can exist without Kṛṣṇa, and Kṛṣṇa is the Lord of everything — this is the basic principle of Kṛṣṇa consciousness. How does the devotee know that everything is the manifestation of Kṛṣṇa's energy? First of all, a Kṛṣṇa conscious person is a philosopher. If he sees a tree, he thinks, "What is this tree?" He then sees that the tree has a material body — just as he has a material body — and that the tree is also a living entity, but due to the tree's past misdeeds, he has obtained such an abominable body that he cannot even move. The tree's body is material, material energy, and the devotee automatically questions, "Whose energy? Kṛṣṇa's energy. Therefore the tree is connected to Kṛṣṇa. Being a living entity, the tree is part and parcel of Kṛṣṇa." In this way, the Kṛṣṇa conscious person does not see the tree, but sees Kṛṣṇa present. That is Kṛṣṇa consciousness: you don't see the tree. You see Kṛṣṇa. That is the perfection of *yoga*, and that is also *samādhi*.

Kṛṣṇa consciousness is the development of love of Kṛṣṇa — a position transcendental even to material liberation. Why does the Kṛṣṇa conscious person take such an account of the tree? Because he has love for Kṛṣṇa. If you love your child and your child is away, you think of him when you see his shoes. You think, "Oh, this is my dear child's shoe." It is not that you love the shoe, but the child. The shoe, however, evokes that love. Similarly, as soon as we see Kṛṣṇa's energy manifested in a living entity, we love that entity because we love Kṛṣṇa. Therefore, if we love Kṛṣṇa, universal love is accounted for. Otherwise "universal love" is nonsensical, because it is not possible to love everybody without loving Kṛṣṇa. If we love Kṛṣṇa, universal love is automatically there. Without being Kṛṣṇa conscious, a person may say, "Here is my British brother, and here is my Indian brother. Now let us eat this cow." Such a person may look on other humans as brothers, but he looks on the cow as food. Is this universal love? A Kṛṣṇa conscious person, however, thinks, "Oh, here is a cow. Here is a dog. They are part and parcel of Kṛṣṇa, but somehow or other they have acquired different bodies. This does not mean that they are not my brothers. How can I kill and eat my brothers?" That is true universal love — rooted in love for Kṛṣṇa. Without such Kṛṣṇa consciousness, there is no question of love at all.

Kṛṣṇa consciousness is the stage beyond self-realisation in which the devotee becomes one with Kṛṣṇa in the sense that Kṛṣṇa becomes everything for the devotee, and the devotee becomes full in loving Kṛṣṇa. An intimate relationship between the Lord and the devotee then exists. In that stage, the living entity attains his immortality. Nor is the Personality of Godhead ever out of sight of the devotee. To merge in Kṛṣṇa is spiritual annihilation. A devotee takes no such risk. It is stated in the *Brahma-saṁhitā* (5.38),

premāñjana-cchurita-bhakti-vilocanena
santaḥ sadaiva hṛdayeṣu vilokayanti
yaṁ śyāmasundaram acintya-guṇa-svarūpaṁ
govindam ādi-puruṣaṁ tam ahaṁ bhajāmi

"I worship the primeval Lord, Govinda, who is always seen by the devotee whose eyes are anointed with the pulp of love. He is seen in His eternal form of Śyāmasundara, situated within the heart of the devotee." One who has developed such a love for Kṛṣṇa sees Śyāmasundara, Kartāmeśāna, always within his heart. At this stage, Lord Kṛṣṇa never disappears from the sight of the devotee, nor does the devotee ever lose sight of the Lord. In the case of a *yogī* who sees the Lord as Paramātmā within the heart, the same applies. Such a *yogī* turns into a pure devotee and cannot bear to live for a moment without seeing the Lord within himself.

This is the real process by which we can see God. God is not our order supplier. We cannot demand, "Come and show Yourself." No, we first have to qualify ourselves. Then we can see God at every moment and everywhere.

sarva-bhūta-sthitaṁ yo māṁ
bhajaty ekatvam āsthitaḥ
sarvathā vartamāno 'pi
sa yogī mayi vartate

"The *yogī* who engages in the worshipable service of the Supersoul, knowing that I and the Supersoul are one, remains always in Me in all circumstances." (Bg. 6.31)

A *yogī* who is practising meditation on the Supersoul sees

within himself the plenary portion of Kṛṣṇa as Viṣṇu — with four hands, holding conchshell, wheel, club and lotus flower. This manifestation of Viṣṇu, which is the *yogī's* object of concentration, is Kṛṣṇa's plenary portion. As stated in *Brahma-saṁhitā* (5.48),

> *yasyaika-niśvasita-kālam athāvalambya*
> *jīvanti loma-vila-jā jagad-aṇḍa-nāthāḥ*
> *viṣṇur mahān sa iha yasya kalā-viśeṣo*
> *govindam ādi-puruṣaṁ tam ahaṁ bhajāmi*

"The Brahmās and other lords of the mundane worlds appear from the pores of Mahā-Viṣṇu and remain alive for the duration of His one exhalation. I adore the primeval Lord, Govinda, for Mahā-Viṣṇu is a portion of His plenary portion." The words *govindam ādi-puruṣaṁ tam ahaṁ bhajāmi* ("I worship Govinda, the primeval Lord") are most important. The word *ādi* means "original", and *puruṣam* means "the Lord as the original male, the original enjoyer". And who is this Govinda whose plenary portion is the Mahā-Viṣṇu? And what is the function of the Mahā-Viṣṇu?

In every universe there is a primary, original living entity known as Brahmā. The life of Brahmā is the life of the universe, and this life exists during only one breathing period (exhalation and inhalation) of the Mahā-Viṣṇu. The Mahā-Viṣṇu lies on the Causal Ocean, and when He exhales, millions of universes issue from His body as bubbles and then develop. When the Mahā-Viṣṇu inhales, these millions of universes return within Him, and this is called the process of annihilation. That, in essence, is the position of these material universes: they come out from the body of the Mahā-Viṣṇu and then again return. In the Ninth Chapter of *Bhagavad-gītā* (9.7) it is also indicated that these material universes are manifest at a certain period and are then annihilated.

sarva-bhūtāni kaunteya
prakṛtiṁ yānti māmikām
kalpa-kṣaye punas tāni
kalpādau visṛjāmy aham

"O son of Kuntī, at the end of the millenium, all material manifestations enter into My nature, and at the beginning of another millenium, by My potency, I create them again." The creation, maintenance, and annihilation of this material cosmic manifestation are completely dependent on the supreme will of the Personality of Godhead. "At the end of the millenium" means at the death of Brahmā. Brahmā lives for one hundred years, and his one day is calculated at 4,300,000,000 of our earthly years. His night is of the same duration. His month consists of thirty such days and nights, and his year of twelve months. After one hundred such years, when Brahmā dies, the devastation or annihilation takes place; this means that the energy manifested by the Supreme Lord is again wound up in Himself. That is, the Mahā-Viṣṇu inhales. Then again, when there is need to manifest the cosmic world, it is done by His will: "Although I am one, I shall become many." This is the Vedic aphorism. He expands Himself in this material energy, and the whole cosmic manifestation again takes place.

Since the entire creation and annihilation of the material universes depend on the exhaling and inhaling of the Mahā-Viṣṇu, we can hardly imagine the magnitude of that Mahā-Viṣṇu. And yet it is said here that this Mahā-Viṣṇu is but a plenary portion of the plenary portion of Kṛṣṇa, who is the original Govinda. The Mahā-Viṣṇu enters into each universe as Garbhodakaśāyī Viṣṇu, and Garbhodakaśāyī Viṣṇu further expands as Kṣīrodakaśāyī Viṣṇu, and it is this Viṣṇu form that enters into the heart of every living entity. In this way, Viṣṇu is manifest throughout the creation. Thus the *yogīs* concentrate their minds on the Kṣīrodakaśāyī Viṣṇu form within the heart. As stated in the last chapter of *Bhagavad-gītā* (18.61),

īśvaraḥ sarva-bhūtānāṁ
hṛd-deśe 'rjuna tiṣṭhati
bhrāmayan sarva-bhūtāni
yantrārūḍhāni māyayā

"The Supreme Lord is situated in everyone's heart, O Arjuna, and is directing the wanderings of all living entities, who are seated as on a machine, made of the material energy."

Thus, according to the yogic process, the *yogī* finds out where the Kṣīrodakaśāyī Viṣṇu is seated within the heart, and when he finds this form there, he concentrates on Him. The *yogī* should know that this Viṣṇu is not different from Kṛṣṇa. Kṛṣṇa in this form of Supersoul is situated in everyone's heart. Furthermore, there is no difference between the innumerable Supersouls present in the innumerable hearts of living entities. For example, there is only one sun in the sky, but this sun may be reflected in millions of buckets of water. Or, one may ask millions and trillions of people, "Where is the sun?" And each will say, "Over my head." The sun is one, but it is reflected countless times. According to the *Vedas,* the living entities are innumerable; there is no possibility of counting them. Just as the sun can be reflected in countless buckets of water, Viṣṇu, the Supreme Personality of Godhead, can live in each and everyone's heart. It is this form that is Kṛṣṇa's plenary portion, and it is this form on which the *yogī* concentrates.

One who is engaged in Kṛṣṇa consciousness is already a perfect *yogī.* In fact, there is no difference between a Kṛṣṇa conscious devotee always engaged in the transcendental loving service of Kṛṣṇa and a perfect *yogī* engaged in meditation on the Supersoul. There is no difference between a *yogī* in *samādhi* (in a trance meditating on the Viṣṇu form) and a Kṛṣṇa conscious person engaged in different activities. The devotee — even though engaged in various activities while in material existence — remains always situated in Kṛṣṇa. This is confirmed in the *Bhakti-rasāmṛta-sindhu* of Śrīla Rūpa Gosvāmī: *nikhilāsv apy avasthāsu jīvan-muktaḥ sa ucyate.* A devotee of the Lord, always acting in Kṛṣṇa consciousness, is automatically liberated. This is also confirmed in the Fourteenth Chapter of *Bhagavad-gītā* (14.26):

māṁ ca yo 'vyabhicāreṇa
bhakti-yogena sevate
sa guṇān samatītyaitān
brahma-bhūyāya kalpate

"One who engages in full devotional service, unfailing in all circumstances, at once transcends the modes of material nature and thus comes to the level of Brahman."

Thus the devotee engaged in unalloyed devotional service has already transcended the material modes of nature. Being situated on the Brahman platform means being liberated. There are three platforms: the bodily, or sensual; the mental; and the spiritual. The spiritual platform is called the Brahman platform, and liberation means being situated on that platform. Being conditioned souls, we are presently situated on the bodily, or sensual, platform. Those who are a little advanced — speculators, philosophers — are situated on the mental platform. Above this is the platform of liberation, of Brahman realisation.

That the devotee, always acting in Kṛṣṇa consciousness,

is automatically situated on the liberated platform of Brahman is also confirmed in the *Nārada-pañcarātra:*

dik-kālādy-anavacchinne
kṛṣṇe ceto vidhāya ca
tan-mayo bhavati kṣipraṁ
jīvo brahmaṇi yojayet

"By concentrating one's attention on the transcendental form of Kṛṣṇa, who is all-pervading and beyond time and space, one becomes absorbed in thinking of Kṛṣṇa and then attains the happy state of transcendental association with Him."

Kṛṣṇa consciousness is the highest stage of trance in *yoga* practice. This very understanding that Kṛṣṇa is present as Paramātmā in everyone's heart makes the *yogī* faultless. The *Vedas* confirm this inconceivable potency of the Lord as follows:

eko 'pi san bahudhā yo 'vabhāti
aiśvaryād rūpaṁ ekaṁ ca sūryavad bahudheyate

"Viṣṇu is one, and yet He is certainly all-pervading. By His inconceivable potency, in spite of His one form, He is present everywhere. As the sun, He appears in many places at once."

ātmaupamyena sarvatra
samaṁ paśyati yo 'rjuna
sukhaṁ vā yadi vā duḥkhaṁ
sa yogī paramo mataḥ

"He is a perfect *yogī* who, by comparison to his own self, sees the true equality of all beings, in both their happiness and their distress, O Arjuna!" (Bg. 6.32) This is true universal vision. It is not that God is sitting in my heart and not in the heart of a dog, cat or cow. *Sarva-bhūtānām* means that He is sitting in the hearts of all living entities, in the human heart and in the ant's heart. The only difference is that cats and dogs cannot realise this. A human being, if he tries to follow the *sāṅkhya-yoga* or *bhakti-yoga* system, is able to understand, and this is the prerogative of human life. If we miss this opportunity, we suffer a great loss, for we have undergone the evolutionary process and have passed through more than eight million species of life in order to get this human form. We should therefore be conscious of this and careful not to miss this opportunity. We have a good body, the human form, and intelligence and civilisation. We should not live like animals and struggle hard for existence but should utilise our time thinking peacefully and understanding our relationship with the Supreme Lord. This is the instruction of *Bhagavad-gītā:* Don't lose this opportunity; utilise it properly.

CHAPTER SEVEN

Yoga for the Modern Age

arjuna uvāca
yo 'yaṁ yogas tvayā proktaḥ
sāmyena madhusūdana
etasyāhaṁ na paśyāmi
cañcalatvāt sthitiṁ sthirām

"Arjuna said: O Madhusūdana, the system of *yoga* which You have summarised appears impractical and unendurable to me, for the mind is restless and unsteady." (Bg. 6.33)

This is the crucial test of the eightfold *aṣṭāṅga-yoga* system expounded herein by Lord Śrī Kṛṣṇa. It has already been explained that one must sit in a certain way and concentrate the mind on the form of Viṣṇu seated within the heart. According to the *aṣṭāṅga-yoga* system, first of all one has to control the senses, follow all the rules and regulations, practise the sitting posture and the breathing process, concentrate the mind on the form of Viṣṇu within the heart, and then become absorbed in that form. There are eight processes in this *aṣṭāṅga-yoga* system, but herein Arjuna says quite frankly that this *aṣṭāṅga-yoga* system is very difficult. Indeed, he says that it "appears impractical and unendurable to me."

Actually, the *aṣṭāṅga-yoga* system is not impractical, for were it impractical, Lord Kṛṣṇa would not have taken so much trouble to describe it. It is not impractical, but it *appears* impractical. What may be impractical for one man may be practical for another. Arjuna is representative of the common man in the sense that he is not a mendicant or a *sannyāsī* or a scholar. He is on the battlefield fighting for his kingdom, and in this sense he is an ordinary man engaged in a worldly activity. He is concerned with earning a livelihood, supporting his family and so on. Arjuna has many problems, just as the common man, and generally this system of *aṣṭāṅga-yoga* is impractical for the ordinary common man. That is the point being made. It is practical for one who has already completely renounced everything and can sit in a secluded, sacred place on the side of a hill or in a cave. But who can do this in this age? Although Arjuna was a great warrior, a member of the royal family and a very advanced person, he proclaims this *yoga* system impractical. And what are we in comparison to Arjuna? If we attempt this system, failure is certain.

Therefore this system of mysticism described by Lord Kṛṣṇa to Arjuna beginning with the words *śucau deśe* and ending with *yogī paramaḥ* is here rejected by Arjuna out of a feeling of inability. As stated before, it is not possible for an ordinary man to leave home and go to a secluded place in the mountains or jungles to practise *yoga* in this age of Kali. The present age is characterised by a bitter struggle for a life of short duration. As Kali-yuga progresses, our life span gets shorter and shorter. Our forefathers lived for a hundred years or more, but now people are dying at the age of sixty or seventy. Gradually the life span will decrease even further. Memory, mercy and other good qualities will also decrease in this age.

In Kali-yuga, people are not serious about self-realisation even by simple, practical means, and what to speak of this difficult *yoga* system, which regulates the mode of living, the manner of sitting, selection of place and detachment of the mind from material engagements. As a practical man, Arjuna thought it was impossible to follow this system of *yoga*, even though he was favourably endowed in many ways. He was not prepared to become a pseudo *yogī* and practise some gymnastic feats. He was not a pretender but a soldier and a family man. Therefore he frankly admitted that for him this system of *yoga* would be a waste of time. Arjuna belonged to the royal family and was highly elevated in terms of numerous qualities; he was a great warrior, he had great longevity and, above all, he was the most intimate friend of Lord Kṛṣṇa, the Supreme Personality of Godhead. Five thousand years ago, when Arjuna was living, the life span was very long. At that time, people used to live up to one thousand years. In the present age of Kali-yuga, the life span is limited to a hundred years; in Dvāpara-yuga, the life span was a thousand years; in Tretā-yuga, the life span was ten thousand years; and in Satya-yuga, the life span was one hundred thousand years. Thus as the *yugas* degenerate, the life span decreases. Even though Arjuna was living at a time when one would live and practise meditation for a thousand years, he still considered this system impossible.

Five thousand years ago, Arjuna had much better facilities than we do now, yet he refused to accept this system of *yoga*. In fact, we do not find any record in history of his practising it at any time. Therefore, this system must be considered generally impossible in this age of Kali. Of course, it may be possible for some very few, rare men, but for the people in general it is an impossible proposal. If this were so five thousand years ago, what of the present day? Those who are imitating this *yoga* system in different so-called schools and societies, although complacent, are certainly wasting their time. They are completely ignorant of the desired goal.

Since this *aṣṭāṅga-yoga* system is considered impossible,

the *bhakti-yoga* system is recommended for everyone. Without training or education, one can automatically participate in *bhakti-yoga.* Even a small child can clap at *kīrtana.* Therefore Lord Caitanya Mahāprabhu has proclaimed *bhakti-yoga* the only system practical for this age.

harer nāma harer nāma
harer nāmaiva kevalam
kalau nāsty eva nāsty eva
nāsty eva gatir anyathā

"In this age of quarrel and hypocrisy the only means of deliverance is chanting the holy name of the Lord. There is no other way. There is no other way. There is no other way." Chanting is very simple, and one will feel the results immediately. *Pratyakṣāvagamaṁ dharmyam.* If we attempt to practise other *yoga* systems, we will remain in darkness; we will not know whether or not we are making progress. In *bhakti-yoga,* one can understand, "Yes, now I am making progress." This is the only *yoga* system by which one can quickly attain self-realisation and liberation in this life. One doesn't have to wait for another lifetime.

cañcalaṁ hi manaḥ kṛṣṇa
pramāthi balavad dṛḍham
tasyāhaṁ nigrahaṁ manye
vāyor iva su-duṣkaram

"For the mind is restless, turbulent, obstinate, and very strong, O Kṛṣṇa, and to subdue it is, it seems to me, more difficult than controlling the wind." (Bg. 6.34) By chanting Hare Kṛṣṇa, one captures the mind immediately. Just by saying the name *Kṛṣṇa* and hearing it, the mind is automatically fixed on Kṛṣṇa. This means that the *yoga* system is immediately attained. The entire *yoga* system aims at concentration on the form of Viṣṇu, and Kṛṣṇa is the original personality from whom all these Viṣṇu forms are expanded. Kṛṣṇa is like the original candle from which all other candles are lit. If one candle is lit, one can light any number of candles, and there is no doubt that each candle is as powerful as the original candle. Nonetheless, one has to recognise the original candle as the original. Similarly, from Kṛṣṇa millions of Viṣṇu forms expand, and each Viṣṇu form is as good as Kṛṣṇa, but Kṛṣṇa remains the original. Thus one who concentrates his mind on Lord Śrī Kṛṣṇa, the original Supreme Personality of Godhead, immediately attains the perfection of *yoga.*

śrī-bhagavān uvāca
asaṁśayaṁ mahā-bāho
mano durnigrahaṁ calam
abhyāsena tu kaunteya
vairāgyeṇa ca gṛhyate

"Lord Śrī Kṛṣṇa said: O mighty-armed son of Kuntī, it is undoubtedly very difficult to curb the restless mind, but it is possible by constant practise and by detachment." (Bg. 6.35) Kṛṣṇa does not say that it is easy. Rather, He admits that it is difficult, but possible by means of constant practise. Constant practise means engaging ourselves in some activities that remind us of Kṛṣṇa. In this society for Kṛṣṇa consciousness we therefore have many activities — *kīrtana,* temple activities, *prasādam,* publications and so on. Everyone is engaged in some activity with Kṛṣṇa at the centre. Therefore whether one is typing for Kṛṣṇa, cooking for Kṛṣṇa, chanting for Kṛṣṇa or distributing literature for Kṛṣṇa, he is in the *yoga* system, and he is also in Kṛṣṇa. We engage in activities just as in material life, but these activities are moulded in such a way that they are directly connected with Kṛṣṇa.

Thus through every activity, Kṛṣṇa consciousness is possible, and perfection in *yoga* follows automatically.

asaṁyatātmanā yogo
duṣprāpa iti me matiḥ
vaśyātmanā tu yatatā
śakyo 'vāptum upāyataḥ

"For one whose mind is unbridled, self-realisation is difficult work. But he whose mind is controlled and who strives by appropriate means is assured of success. That is My opinion." (Bg. 6.36) The Supreme Personality of Godhead declares that one who does not accept the proper treatment to detach the mind from material engagement can hardly achieve success in self-realisation. Trying to practise *yoga* while engaging the mind in material enjoyment is like trying to ignite a fire while pouring water on it. Similarly, *yoga* practice without mental control is a waste of time. I may sit down to meditate and focus my mind on Kṛṣṇa, and that is very commendable, but there are many *yoga* societies that teach their students to concentrate on the void or on some colour. That is, they do not recommend concentration on the form of Viṣṇu. Trying to concentrate the mind on the impersonal or the void is very difficult and troublesome. It is stated by Śrī Kṛṣṇa in the Twelfth Chapter of *Bhagavad-gītā* (12.5).

kleśo 'dhikataras teṣām
avyaktāsakta-cetasām
avyaktā hi gatir duḥkhaṁ
dehavadbhir avāpyate

"For those whose minds are attached to the unmanifested, impersonal feature of the Supreme, advancement is very troublesome. To make progress in that discipline is always difficult for those who are embodied."

In the temple, the devotee tries to concentrate on the form of Kṛṣṇa. Concentrating on nothingness, on void, is very difficult, and naturally the mind is very flickering. Therefore instead of concentrating on the void, the mind searches out something else. The mind must be engaged in thinking of something, and if it is not thinking of Kṛṣṇa, it must be thinking of *māyā.* Therefore, pseudomeditation on the impersonal void is simply a waste of time. Such a show of *yoga* practice may be materially lucrative, but useless as far as spiritual realisation is concerned. I may open a class in yogic meditation and charge people money for sitting down and pressing their nose this way and that, but if my students do not attain the real goal of *yoga* practice, they have wasted their time and money, and I have cheated them.

Therefore one has to concentrate his mind steadily and constantly on the form of Viṣṇu, and that is called *samādhi.* In Kṛṣṇa consciousness, the mind is controlled by engaging it constantly in the transcendental loving service of the Lord. Unless one is engaged in Kṛṣṇa consciousness, he cannot steadily control the mind. A Kṛṣṇa conscious person easily achieves the result of *yoga* practice without separate endeavour, but a *yoga* practitioner cannot achieve success without becoming Kṛṣṇa conscious.

CHAPTER EIGHT

Failure and Success in Yoga

Suppose I give up my business, my ordinary occupation, and begin to practise *yoga*, real *yoga*, as explained herein by Lord Śrī Kṛṣṇa. Suppose I practise, and somehow or other I fail; I cannot properly complete the process. What, then, is the result? This is Arjuna's very next question.

arjuna uvāca
ayatiḥ śraddhayopeto
yogāc calita-mānasaḥ
aprāpya yoga-saṁsiddhiṁ
kāṁ gatiṁ kṛṣṇa gacchati

"Arjuna said: O Kṛṣṇa, what is the destination of the unsuccessful transcendentalist, who in the beginning takes to the process of self-realisation with faith but who later desists due to worldly-mindedness and thus does not attain perfection in mysticism?" (Bg. 6.37)

The path of self-realisation, of mysticism, is described in the *Bhagavad-gītā*. The basic principle of self-realisation is knowing that "I am not this material body but am different from it, and my happiness is in eternal life, bliss, and knowledge." Before arriving at the point of self-realisation, one must take it for granted that he is not this body. That lesson is taught in the very beginning of *Bhagavad-gītā:* the living entity is not this material body but something different, and his happiness is in eternal life.

Clearly, this life is not eternal. The perfection of *yoga* means attaining a blissful, eternal life full of knowledge. All *yoga* systems should be executed with that goal in mind. It is not that one attends *yoga* classes to reduce fat or to keep the body fit for sense gratification. This is not the goal of *yoga,* but people are taught this way because they want to be cheated. Actually, if you undergo any exercise programme, your body will be kept fit. There are many systems of bodily exercise — weight lifting and other sports — and they help keep the body fit, reduce fat and help the digestive system. Therefore there is no need to practise *yoga* for these purposes. The real purpose for practising *yoga* is to realise that I am not this body. I want eternal happiness, complete knowledge and eternal life — that is the ultimate end of the true *yoga* system.

The goal of *yoga* is transcendental, beyond both body and mind. Self-realisation is sought by three methods: (1) the path of knowledge (*jñāna*); (2) the path of the eightfold system; or (3) the path of *bhakti-yoga.* In each of these processes, one has to realise the constitutional position of the living entity, his relationship with God and the activities whereby he can reestablish the lost link and achieve the highest perfectional stage of Kṛṣṇa consciousness. Following any of the above-mentioned three methods, one is sure to reach the supreme goal sooner or later. This was asserted by the Lord in the Second Chapter: even a little endeavour on the transcendental path offers a great hope for deliverance.

Of these three methods, the path of *bhakti-yoga* is especially suitable for this age, because it is the most direct method of God realisation. To be doubly assured, Arjuna is asking Lord Kṛṣṇa to confirm His former statement. One may sincerely accept the path of self-realisation, but the process of cultivation of knowledge (*jñāna*) and the practise of the eightfold *yoga* system are generally very difficult for this age. Therefore, despite constant endeavour, one may fail for many reasons. First of all, one may not be actually following the process, the rules and regulations. To pursue the transcendental path is more or less to declare war on the illusory energy. When we accept any process of self-realisation, we are actually declaring war against *māyā*, illusion, and *māyā* is certain to place many difficulties before us. Therefore, there is a chance of failure, but one has to become very steady. Whenever a person tries to escape the clutches of the illusory energy, she tries to defeat the practitioner by various allurements. A conditioned soul is already allured by the modes of material energy, and there is every chance of being allured again, even while performing transcendental disciplines. This is called *yogāc calita-mānasaḥ:* deviation from the transcendental path. Arjuna is inquisitive to know the results of deviation from the path of self-realisation.

As stated in *Bhagavad-gītā* (6.37), quoted above, *yogāt* means "from the practise of *yoga*", *calita* means "diversion" and *mānasaḥ* means "mind". So there is every chance for the mind to be diverted from *yoga* practice. We all have some experience of trying to concentrate by reading a book, and our mind is so disturbed that it does not allow us to concentrate on the book.

Actually, Arjuna is asking a very important question, for one is subject to failure in all types of *yoga* — be it the eightfold *yoga* system, the *jñāna-yoga* system of speculative philosophy or the *bhakti-yoga* system of devotional service. Failure is possible on any of these paths, and the results of failure are clearly explained by Śrī Kṛṣṇa Himself in the following dialogue with Arjuna (Bg. 6.38-44). Arjuna, continuing his enquiry, asks,

kaccin nobhaya-vibhraṣṭaś
chinnābhram iva naśyati
apratiṣṭho mahā-bāho
vimūḍho brahmaṇaḥ pathi

"O mighty-armed Kṛṣṇa, does not such a man, who is bewildered from the path of transcendence, fall away from both spiritual and material success and perish like a riven cloud, with no position in any sphere?"

etan me saṁśayaṁ kṛṣṇa
chettum arhasy aśeṣataḥ
tvad-anyaḥ saṁśayasyāsya
chettā na hy upapadyate

"This is my doubt, O Kṛṣṇa, and I ask You to dispel it completely. But for You, no one is to be found who can destroy this doubt."

śrī-bhagavān uvāca
pārtha naiveha nāmutra
vināśas tasya vidyate
na hi kalyāṇa-kṛt kaścid
durgatiṁ tāta gacchati

"The Supreme Personality of Godhead said: Son of Pṛthā, a transcendentalist engaged in auspicious activities does not meet with destruction either in this world or in the spiritual world; one who does good, My friend, is never overcome by evil."

prāpya puṇya-kṛtāṁ lokān
uṣitvā śāśvatīḥ samāḥ
śucīnāṁ śrīmatāṁ gehe
yoga-bhraṣṭo 'bhijāyate

"The unsuccessful *yogī,* after many, many years of enjoyment on the planets of the pious living entities, is born into a family of righteous people, or into a family of rich aristocracy."

atha vā yoginām eva
kule bhavati dhīmatām
etad dhi durlabhataraṁ
loke janma yad īdṛśam

"Or, if unsuccessful after long practice of *yoga,* he takes his birth in a family of transcendentalists who are surely great in wisdom. Certainly, such a birth is rare in this world."

tatra taṁ buddhi-saṁyogaṁ
labhate paurva-dehikam
yatate ca tato bhūyaḥ
saṁsiddhau kuru-nandana

"On taking such a birth, he revives the divine consciousness of his previous life, and he tries to make further progress in order to achieve complete success, O son of Kuru."

pūrvābhyāsena tenaiva
hriyate hy avaśo 'pi saḥ
jijñāsur api yogasya
śabda-brahmātivartate

"By virtue of the divine consciousness of his previous life, he automatically becomes attracted to the yogic principles — even without seeking them. Such an inquisitive transcendentalist, stands always above the ritualistic principles of the scriptures."

Purification of consciousness is the purpose of this Kṛṣṇa consciousness movement. Presently we are preparing this divine consciousness, for our consciousness goes with us at the time of death. Consciousness is carried from the body just as the aroma of a flower is carried by the air. When we die, this material body composed of five elements — earth, water, air, fire and ether — decomposes, and the gross materials return to the elements. Or, as the Christian Bible says, "Dust thou art, and unto dust thou shalt return." In some societies the body is burned, in others it is buried and in others it is thrown to animals. In India, the Hindus burn the body, and thus the body is transformed into ashes. Ash is simply another form of earth. Christians bury the body, and after some time in the grave, the body eventually turns to dust, which again, like ash, is another form of earth. There are other societies — like the Parsee community in India — that neither burn nor bury the body but throw it to the vultures, and the vultures immediately come to eat the body, and then the body is eventually transformed into stool. So in any case, this beautiful body, which we are soaping and caring for so nicely, will eventually turn into either stool, ashes or dust.

At death, the finer elements (mind, intelligence and ego), which, combined, are called consciousness, carry the small particle of spirit soul to another body to suffer or enjoy, according to one's work. Our consciousness is moulded by our work. If we associate with stool, our consciousness, which is like the air, will carry the aroma of stool, and thus at the time of death will transport us to an undesirable body. Or, if the consciousness passes over roses, it carries the aroma of roses, and thus we are transported to a body wherein we can enjoy the results of our previous work. If we train ourselves to work in Kṛṣṇa consciousness, our consciousness will carry us to Kṛṣṇa. Different types of body are developed according to consciousness; therefore, if we train our consciousness according to the yogic principles, we will attain a body wherein we can practise *yoga.* We will get good parents and a chance to practise the *yoga* system, and automatically we will be able to revive the Kṛṣṇa consciousness practised in our previous body. Therefore it is stated in this last verse, "By virtue of the divine consciousness of his previous life, he automatically becomes attracted to the yogic principles — even without seeking them." Therefore, our present duty is to cultivate divine consciousness. If we want divine life, spiritual elevation and eternal, blissful life, full of knowledge — in other words, if we want to go back home, back to Godhead — we have to train ourselves in divine consciousness, or Kṛṣṇa consciousness.

This can be easily done through association (*saṅgāt sañjāyate kāmaḥ*). Through divine association, our consciousness is made divine, and through demoniac association, our consciousness is made demoniac. Therefore, our consciousness must be trained to be divine through the proper association of those in Kṛṣṇa consciousness. That is the duty of one in this human form, a form that gives us a chance to make our next life completely divine. To attain this end, we should try to contact those who are developing their divine consciousness.

prayatnād yatamānas tu
yogī saṁśuddha-kilbiṣaḥ
aneka-janma-saṁsiddhas
tato yāti parāṁ gatim

"And when the *yogī* engages himself with sincere endeavour in making further progress, being washed of all contaminations, then ultimately, achieving perfection after many, many births of practice, he attains the supreme goal." (Bg. 6.45) As indicated in this verse, making progress is a question of practise. When a child is born, he neither knows how to smoke nor how to drink, but through association he becomes a drunkard or a smoker. Association is the most important factor. *Saṅgāt sañjāyate kāmaḥ.* For instance, there are many business associations, and by becoming a member of certain associations, one's business flourishes. In any endeavour, association is very important. For the development of divine consciousness, we have established the International Society for Krishna Consciousness, in which the methods of attaining divine consciousness are taught. In this society we invite everyone to come and chant Hare Kṛṣṇa. This process is not difficult, and even children can participate. No previous qualifications are necessary; one doesn't need a master's degree or doctorate. Our invitation to everyone is to join this association and become Kṛṣṇa conscious.

The Supreme Lord, God, is pure, and His kingdom is also pure. If one wants to enter His kingdom, he must also be pure. This is very natural; if we want to enter a particular society, we must meet certain qualifications. If we want to return home, back to Godhead, there is a qualification we must meet — we must not be materially contaminated. And what is this contamination? Unrestricted sense gratification. If we can free ourselves from the material contamination of sense gratification, we can become eligible to enter the kingdom of God. That process of freeing ourselves, of washing ourselves of this contamination, is called the *yoga* system. As stated before, *yoga* does not mean sitting down for fifteen minutes, meditating, and then continuing with sense gratification. To be cured of a certain disease, we must follow the prescriptions of a physician. In this Sixth Chapter of *Bhagavad-gītā,* the process of *yoga* is recommended, and we have to follow the prescribed methods in order to be freed from material contamination. If we succeed in doing so, we can link up, or connect, with the Supreme.

Kṛṣṇa consciousness is a method for connecting directly with the Supreme. This is the special gift of Lord Caitanya Mahāprabhu. Not only is this method direct and immediate, but it is also practical. Although many people entering this society have no qualifications, they have become highly advanced in Kṛṣṇa consciousness simply by coming in contact with the society. In this age, life is very short, and a *yoga* process that takes a long time will not help the general populace. In Kali-yuga, people are all so unfortunate, and association is very bad. Therefore, this process of directly contacting the Supreme is recommended—*hari-nāma.* Kṛṣṇa is present in the form of His transcendental name, and we can contact Him immediately by hearing His name. Simply by hearing the name *Kṛṣṇa* we immediately become freed from material contamination.

As stated in the Seventh Chapter of *Bhagavad-gītā* (7.28),

yeṣāṁ tv anta-gataṁ pāpaṁ
janānāṁ puṇya-karmaṇām
te dvandva-moha-nirmuktā
bhajante māṁ dṛḍha-vratāḥ

"Persons who have acted piously in previous lives and in this life, whose sinful actions are completely eradicated are freed from the duality of delusion, and they engage themselves in My service with determination." It is stressed herein that one must be completely fixed in Kṛṣṇa consciousness, devoid of duality, and must execute only pious activities. Because the mind is flickering, dualities will always come. One is always wondering, "Shall I become Kṛṣṇa conscious, or should I engage in another consciousness?" These problems are always there, but if one is advanced by virtue of pious activities executed in a previous life, his consciousness will be steadily fixed, and he will resolve, "I must become Kṛṣṇa conscious."

Whether we acted piously in this life or a previous life really doesn't matter. This chanting of Hare Kṛṣṇa is so potent that through it we will immediately be purified. We should have the determination, however, not to become implicated in further impious activities. Therefore, for those who want to be initiated in this society for Kṛṣṇa consciousness, there are four principles: no illicit sex, no intoxication, no meat-eating and no gambling. We don't say, "No sex." But we do say, "No illicit sex." If you want sex, get married and have Kṛṣṇa conscious children. "No intoxication" means not even taking tea or coffee — to say nothing of other intoxicants. And there is no gambling and no meat-eating (including fish and eggs). Simply by following these four basic rules and regulations, one becomes immediately uncontaminated. No further endeavour is necessary. As soon as one joins this Kṛṣṇa consciousness movement and follows these rules and regulations, material contamination is immediately removed, but one must be careful not to be contaminated again. Therefore these rules and regulations should be followed carefully.

Material contamination begins with these four bad habits, and if we manage to check them, there is no question of contamination. Therefore, as soon as we take to Kṛṣṇa consciousness, we become free. However, we should not think that because Kṛṣṇa consciousness makes us free, we can again indulge in these four bad habits and get free by chanting. That is cheating, and that will not be allowed. Once we are freed, we should not allow ourselves to become contaminated again. One should not think, "I shall drink or have illicit sex and then chant and make myself free." According to some religious processes, it is said that one can commit all kinds of sin and then go to church, confess to a priest and be freed of all sin. Therefore people are sinning and confessing and sinning and confessing over and over again.

But this is not the process of Kṛṣṇa consciousness. If you are freed, that's all right, but don't do it again. After all, what is the purpose of confession? If you confess, "I have committed these sinful activities," why should you commit them again? If a thief confesses that he has been pickpocketing, he is freed of his sin by virtue of his confession, but does this mean that he should go out again and pick pockets? This requires a little intelligence. One should not think that because by confessing one becomes freed, he should continue to commit sinful activities, confess again, and again become freed. That is not the purpose of confession.

We should therefore understand that if we indulge in unrestricted sinful activities, we become contaminated. We should be careful to have sex only according to the rules and regulations, to eat only food that has been prescribed and properly offered, to defend as Kṛṣṇa advised Arjuna — for the right cause. In this way we can avoid contamination and purify our life. If we can continue to live a pure life until the time of death, we will surely be transferred to the kingdom of God. When one is fully in Kṛṣṇa consciousness, he does not return to this material world when he gives up his body. This is stated in the Fourth Chapter (Bg. 4.9).

janma karma ca me divyam
evaṁ yo vetti tattvataḥ
tyaktvā dehaṁ punar janma
naiti mām eti so 'rjuna

"One who knows the transcendental nature of My appearance and activities does not, upon leaving the body, take his birth again in this material world, but attains My eternal abode, O Arjuna."

The unsuccessful *yogī* returns to a good family or to a righteous, rich or aristocratic family, but if one is situated in perfect Kṛṣṇa consciousness, he does not return again. He attains Goloka Vṛndāvana in the eternal spiritual sky. We should be determined not to come back to this material world again, because even if we attain a good birth in a rich or aristocratic family, we can degrade ourselves again by improperly utilising our good chance. Why take this risk? It is better to complete the process of Kṛṣṇa consciousness in this life. It is very simple and not at all difficult. We only have to keep thinking of Kṛṣṇa; then we will be assured that our next birth will be in the spiritual sky, in Goloka Vṛndāvana, in the kingdom of God.

tapasvibhyo 'dhiko yogī
jñānibhyo 'pi mato 'dhikaḥ
karmibhyaś cādhiko yogī
tasmād yogī bhavārjuna

"A *yogī* is greater than the ascetic, greater than the empiricist and greater than the fruitive worker. Therefore, O Arjuna, in all circumstances, be a *yogī*." (Bg. 6.46) There are different gradations of life within this material world, but if one lives according to the yogic principle, especially the principles of *bhakti-yoga,* one is living the most perfect life possible. Therefore Kṛṣṇa is telling Arjuna, "My dear friend Arjuna, in all circumstances be a *yogī* and remain a *yogī*."

yoginām api sarveṣāṁ
mad-gatenāntar-ātmanā
śraddhāvān bhajate yo māṁ
sa me yuktatamo mataḥ

"And of all *yogīs,* the one with great faith who always abides in Me, thinks of Me within himself, and renders transcendental loving service to Me, is most intimately united with Me in *yoga* and is the highest of all." (Bg. 6.47) Here it is clearly stated that there are many types of *yogīs* — *aṣṭāṅga-yogīs, haṭha-yogīs, jñāna-yogīs, karma-yogīs* and *bhakti-yogīs* — and that of all the *yogīs*, "he who always abides in Me" is said to be the greatest of all. "In Me" means in Kṛṣṇa; that is, the greatest *yogī* is always in Kṛṣṇa consciousness. Such a *yogī* "abides in Me with great faith, worshipping Me in transcendental loving service, is most intimately united with Me in *yoga*, and is the highest of all." This is the prime instruction of this Sixth Chapter on *sāṅkhya-yoga:* if one wants to attain the highest platform of *yoga*, one must remain in Kṛṣṇa consciousness.

In Sanskrit, the word *bhajate*, with its root *bhaj* (*bhaj-dhātu*) means "to render service". But who renders service to Kṛṣṇa unless he is a devotee of Kṛṣṇa? In this society of Kṛṣṇa consciousness, devotees are rendering service without payment, out of love for Kṛṣṇa. They can render service elsewhere and get paid hundreds of pounds a month, but this service rendered here is loving service (*bhaj*), based on love of Godhead. Devotees render service in many ways — gardening, typing, cooking, cleaning, etc. All activities are connected with Kṛṣṇa, and therefore Kṛṣṇa consciousness is prevailing twenty-four hours a day. That is the highest type of *yoga*. That is "worshipping Me in transcendental loving service". As stated before, the perfection of *yoga* is keeping one's consciousness in contact with Viṣṇu, or Kṛṣṇa, the Supreme Lord. We are not simply boasting that even a child can be the highest *yogī* simply by participating in Kṛṣṇa consciousness; no, this is the verdict of authorised scripture — *Bhagavad-gītā*. These words are not our creation but are specifically stated by Lord Śrī Kṛṣṇa, the Supreme Personality of Godhead Himself.

Actually, worship and service are somewhat different.

Worship implies some motive. I worship a friend or an important man because if I can please that person, I may derive some profit. Those who worship the demigods worship for some ulterior purpose, and that is condemned in the Seventh Chapter of *Bhagavad-gītā* (7.20):

kāmais tais tair hṛta-jñānāḥ
prapadyante 'nya-devatāḥ
taṁ taṁ niyamam āsthāya
prakṛtyā niyatāḥ svayā

"Those whose intelligence has been stolen by material desires surrender unto demigods and follow the particular rules and regulations of worship according to their own natures." Those who are bewildered by lust worship the demigods with a motive; therefore, when we speak of worship, some motive is implied. Service, however, is different, for in service there is no motive. Service is rendered out of love, just as a mother renders service to her child out of love only. Everyone can neglect that child, but the mother cannot, because love is present. *Bhaj-dhātu* is similar in that there is no question of motive, but service is rendered out of pure love. That is the perfection of Kṛṣṇa consciousness.

This is also the recommendation of *Śrīmad-Bhāgavatam* (1.2.6):

sa vai puṁsāṁ paro dharmo
yato bhaktir adhokṣaje
ahaituky apratihatā
yayātmā suprasīdati

"The supreme occupation [*dharma*] for all humanity is that by which men can attain to loving devotional service unto the transcendent Lord. Such devotional service must be unmotivated and uninterrupted to completely satisfy the self." *Yato bhaktir adhokṣaje.* The word *bhakti* comes from the same root as *bhaj.* The test of a first-class religion is whether or not we are developing our love for God. If we practise religion with some ulterior motive, hoping to fulfil our material necessities, our religion is not first class but third class. It must be understood that first-class religion is that by which we can develop our love of Godhead. *Ahaituky apratihatā.* This perfect religion should be executed without ulterior motive or impediment. That is the *yoga* system recommended in the *Śrīmad-Bhāgavatam* and in this Sixth Chapter of the *Bhagavad-gītā.* That is the system of Kṛṣṇa consciousness.

Kṛṣṇa consciousness is not rendered with some motive in mind. The devotees are not serving Kṛṣṇa in order that He supply them this or that. For a devotee there is no scarcity. One should not think that by becoming Kṛṣṇa conscious, one becomes poor. No. If Kṛṣṇa is there, everything is there, because Kṛṣṇa is everything. But this does not mean that we should try to conduct business with Kṛṣṇa, demanding, "Kṛṣṇa give me this. Give me that." Kṛṣṇa knows better than we do, and He knows our motives. A child does not make demands of his parents, saying, "Dear father, give me this. Give me that." Since the father knows his child's necessities, there is no need for the child to ask. Similarly, it is not a very good idea to ask God to give us this or that. Why should we ask? If God is all-knowing and all-powerful, He knows our wants, our necessities, and can supply them. This is confirmed in the *Vedas. Eko bahūnāṁ yo vidadhāti kāmān:* "The single one almighty God is supplying all necessities to millions and trillions of living entities." Therefore, we should not demand anything of God, because our demands are already met. The supplies are already there.

We should simply try to love God. Even cats and dogs are receiving their necessities without going to church and petitioning God. If a cat or dog receives its necessities without making demands, why should the devotee not receive what he needs? Therefore we should not demand anything from God but should simply try to love Him. Then everything will be fulfiled, and we will have attained the highest platform of *yoga.*

We can actually see how the various parts of the body serve the body. If I have an itch, the fingers immediately scratch. If I want to see something, the eyes immediately look. If I want to go somewhere, the legs immediately take me. As I receive service from the different parts of my body, God receives service from all parts of His creation. God is not meant to serve. If the limbs of the body serve the entire body, the parts of the body automatically receive energy. Similarly, if we serve Kṛṣṇa, we automatically receive all necessities, all energy.

Śrīmad-Bhāgavatam confirms that we are all parts and parcels of the Supreme. If a part of the body cannot regularly render service, it gives pain to the body, and if a person does not render service to the Supreme Lord, he is simply giving pain and trouble to the Supreme Lord. Therefore such a person has to suffer, just as a criminal has to suffer when he does not abide by the laws of the state. Such a criminal may think, "I'm a very good man," but because he is violating the laws of the state, he is giving the government trouble, and consequently the government puts him in prison. When living entities give the Supreme Lord trouble, the Lord comes, collects them together and puts them in this material world. In essence, He says, "You live here. You are all disturbing the creation; therefore you are criminals and have to live in this material world." *Sthānād bhraṣ-*

ṭāḥ patanty adhaḥ: "One falls down from his constitutional position." If a finger is diseased, it has to be amputated lest it pollute the entire body. Having rebelled against the principles of God consciousness, we are cut off from our original position. We have fallen. In order to regain our original position, we must resume rendering service unto the Supreme Lord. That is the perfect cure. Otherwise we will continue to suffer pain, and God will suffer pain because of us. If I am a father, and my son is not good, I suffer, and my son suffers also. Similarly, we are all sons of God, and when we cause God pain, we are also pained. The best course is to revive our original Kṛṣṇa consciousness and engage in the Lord's service. That is our natural life, and that is possible in the spiritual sky, Goloka Vṛndāvana.

The word *avajānanti* actually means "to neglect". This means thinking, "What is God? I am God. Why should I serve God?" This is just like a criminal thinking, "What is this government? I can manage my own affairs. I don't care for the government." This is called *avajānanti.* We may speak in this way, but the police department is there to punish us. Similarly, material nature is here to punish us with the threefold miseries. These miseries are meant for those rascals who *avajānanti,* who don't care for God or who take the meaning of *God* cheaply, saying, "I am God. You are God."

Thus the general progress of *yoga* is gradual. First one practises *karma-yoga,* which refers to ordinary, fruitive activity. Ordinary activities include sinful activities, but *karma-yoga* excludes such activities. *Karma-yoga* refers only to good, pious activities, or those actions which are prescribed. After performing *karma-yoga,* one comes to the platform of *jñāna-yoga,* knowledge. From the platform of knowledge, one attains to this *aṣṭāṅga-yoga,* the eightfold *yoga* system — *dhyāna, dhāraṇā, prāṇāyāma, āsana,* etc. — and from *aṣṭ-*

aṅga-yoga, as one concentrates on Viṣṇu, one comes to the point of *bhakti-yoga. Bhakti-yoga* is the perfectional stage, and if one practises Kṛṣṇa consciousness, one attains this stage from the very beginning. That is the direct route.

If one practises *jñāna-yoga* and thinks that he has attained the ultimate, he is mistaken. He has to make further progress. If we are on a staircase and have to reach the top floor, which is the hundredth floor, we are mistaken if we think we have arrived when we are on the thirtieth floor. As stated before, the whole *yoga* system may be likened to a staircase, connecting or linking us to God. In order to attain the ultimate, the Supreme Personality of Godhead, we must go to the highest platform, and that is *bhakti-yoga.*

But why walk up all these steps if we have a chance to take an lift? By means of an lift, we can reach the top in a matter of seconds. *Bhakti-yoga* is this lift, the direct process by which we can reach the top in a matter of seconds. We can go step by step, following all the other *yoga* systems, or we can go directly. Since in this age of Kali-yuga people have short life spans and are always disturbed and anxious, Lord Caitanya Mahāprabhu, by His causeless mercy, has given us the lift by which we can come immediately to the platform of *bhakti-yoga.* That direct means is the chanting of Hare Kṛṣṇa, and that is the special gift of Lord Caitanya Mahāprabhu. Therefore Rūpa Gosvāmī offers respects to Lord Caitanya Mahāprabhu, *namo mahā-vadānyāya kṛṣṇa-prema-pradāya te:* "Oh, You are the most munificent incarnation because You are directly giving love of Kṛṣṇa. To attain pure love of Kṛṣṇa, one has to pass through so many stages of *yoga,* but You are giving this love directly. Therefore You are the most munificent."

As stated in the Eighteenth Chapter of *Bhagavad-gītā* (18.55),

bhaktyā mām abhijānāti
yāvān yaś cāsmi tattvataḥ
tato māṁ tattvato jñātvā
viśate tad-anantaram

"One can understand the Supreme Personality as He is only by devotional service. And when one is in full consciousness of the Supreme Lord by such devotion, he can enter into the kingdom of God." In the other *yoga* systems, there must be a mixture of *bhakti,* but *bhakti-yoga* is unadulterated devotion. It is service without a motive. Generally people pray with some motive in mind, but we should pray only for further engagement in devotional service. Lord Caitanya Mahāprabhu has taught us that when we pray we should not pray for anything material. In the beginning, we cited Lord Caitanya Mahāprabhu's perfect prayer:

na dhanaṁ na janaṁ na sundarīṁ
kavitāṁ vā jagad-īśa kāmaye
mama janmani janmanīśvare
bhavatād bhaktir ahaitukī tvayi

"O Almighty Lord, I have no desire to accumulate wealth, nor to enjoy beautiful women. Nor do I want any number of followers. What I want only is the causeless mercy of Your devotional service in my life, birth after birth." (*Śikṣāṣṭaka* 4) In this verse, Caitanya Mahāprabhu addresses the Supreme Lord as Jagadīśa. *Jagat* means "universe", and *īśa* means "controller". The Supreme Lord is the controller of the universe, and this can be understood by anyone; therefore Caitanya Mahāprabhu addresses the Supreme Lord as Jagadīśa instead of Kṛṣṇa or Rāma. In the material world we find many controllers, so it is logical that there is a controller of the entire universe. Caitanya Mahāprabhu does not pray for wealth, followers or beautiful women, because these are material requests. Usually, people want to be very great leaders within this material world. Someone tries to become a very rich man like Ford or Rockefeller, or someone else tries to become prime minister or some great leader that many thousands of people will follow. These are all material demands: "Give me money. Give me followers. Give me a nice wife." Lord Caitanya Mahāprabhu refuses to make such materialistic requests. He frankly says, "I don't want any of these things." He even says, *mama janmani janmanīśvare.* That is, He's not even asking for liberation. Just as the materialists have their demands, the *yogīs* demand liberation. But Caitanya Mahāprabhu does not want anything of this nature. Then why is He a devotee? Why is He worshipping Kṛṣṇa? "I simply want to engage in Your service birth after birth." He does not even pray for an end to birth, old age, disease and death. There are no demands whatsoever, for this is the highest platform, the stage of *bhakti-yoga.*

Chanting Hare Kṛṣṇa is also asking the Lord, "Please engage me in Your service." This is the *mantra* taught by Caitanya Mahāprabhu Himself. *Hare* refers to the energy of the Lord, and *Kṛṣṇa* and *Rāma* are names for the Lord Himself. When we chant Hare Kṛṣṇa, we are asking Kṛṣṇa to please engage us in His service. This is because our entire material disease is due to our having forgotten to serve God. In illusion, we are thinking, "I am God. What is the other God that I have to serve? I myself am God." Ultimately, that is the only disease, the last snare of illusion. First of all, a person tries to be prime minister, president, Rockefeller, Ford, this and that, and when one fails or attains such a post and is still unhappy, he wants to become God. That is like becoming an even higher president. When I understand that the presidency does not afford me eternal bliss and knowledge, I demand the highest presidency. I demand to become

God. In any case, the demand is there, and this demand is our disease. In illusion, we are demanding to be the highest, but the process of *bhakti-yoga* is just the opposite. We want to become servants, servants of the servants of the Lord. There is no question of demanding to become the Lord; we just want to serve. That's all.

Our original nature is rooted in service, and wanting to serve is the crucial test for the devotee. We may not realise it, but in this material world we are also serving. If we want to become president, we have to make so many promises to the voters. In other words, the president has to say, "I'll give the people my service." Unless he promises to serve his country, there is no question of his becoming president. So even if one is the most exalted leader, his position is to render service. This is very difficult for people to understand. Despite becoming the highest executive in the land, one has to give service to the people. If that service is not given, one is likely to be usurped, fired or killed. In the material world, service is very dangerous. If there is a little discrepancy in one's service, one is immediately fired. In America when the people did not like the service that President Nixon was rendering, they forced him to resign. Some people disagreed with President Kennedy, and he was killed. Similarly, in India, Gandhi was also killed because some people did not like the way he was rendering service. This is always the position in the material world; therefore one should be intelligent enough to decide to cease rendering service for material motives. We must render service to the Supreme Lord, and that rendering of service is our perfection.

We have formed this International Society for Krishna Consciousness in order to teach people what they have forgotten. In this material world, we have forgotten the service of Rādhā-Kṛṣṇa; therefore we have become servants of *māyā,* the senses. Therefore, in this society we are saying,

"You are serving your senses. Now just turn your service to Rādhā and Kṛṣṇa, and you will be happy. You have to render service — either to *māyā* [illusion], the senses or to Śrī Śrī Rādhā-Kṛṣṇa."

In this world, everyone is serving the senses, but people are not satisfied. No one can be satisfied, because the senses are always demanding more gratification, and this means that we are constantly having to serve the senses. In any case, our position as servant remains the same. It is a question of whether we want to be happy in our service. It is the verdict of *Bhagavad-gītā* and the other Vedic scriptures that we will never be happy trying to serve our senses, for they are only sources of misery. Therefore Lord Caitanya Mahāprabhu prays to be situated in Kṛṣṇa's service. He also prays,

ayi nanda-tanuja kiṅkaraṁ
patitaṁ māṁ viṣame bhavāmbudhau
kṛpayā tava pāda-paṅkaja-
sthita-dhūlī-sadṛśaṁ vicintaya

"O son of Mahārāja Nanda [Kṛṣṇa], I am Your eternal servitor, yet somehow or other I have fallen into the ocean of birth and death. Please pick me up from this ocean of death and place me as one of the atoms at Your lotus feet." (*Śikṣāṣṭaka* 5) This is another way of asking Kṛṣṇa to engage us in His service.

Loving devotional service can only be rendered to the personal form of Kṛṣṇa, Śyāmasundara. The impersonalists emphasise the *viśva-rūpa*, the universal form exhibited in the Eleventh Chapter of *Bhagavad-gītā*, but it is stated therein (11.21) that the demigods are very much afraid of this form, and Arjuna says,

adṛṣta-pūrvaṁ hṛṣito 'smi dṛṣṭvā
bhayena ca pravyathitaṁ mano me

tad eva me darśaya deva rūpaṁ
prasīda deveśa jagan-nivāsa

"After seeing this universal form, which I have never seen before, I am gladdened, but at the same time my mind is disturbed with fear. Therefore please bestow Your grace upon me and reveal again Your form as the Personality of Godhead [Kṛṣṇa, or Śyāmasundara], O Lord of lords, O abode of the universe." (Bg. 11.45) There is no question of loving the *viśva-rūpa.* If Kṛṣṇa comes before you in the *viśva-rūpa* form, you will be so filled with fear that you will forget your love. So don't be eager like the impersonalists to see the *viśva-rūpa* form; just render loving service to Śyāmasundara, Kṛṣṇa.

We have more or less seen Kṛṣṇa as the *viśva-rūpa* during wartime in Calcutta in 1942. There was a siren, and we ran into a shelter, and the bombing began. In this way, we were seeing that *viśva-rūpa,* and I was thinking, "Of course, this is also just another form of Kṛṣṇa. But this is not a very lovable form." A devotee wants to love Kṛṣṇa in His original form, and this *viśva-rūpa* is not His original form. Being omnipotent, Kṛṣṇa can appear in any form, but His lovable form is that of Kṛṣṇa, Śyāmasundara. Although a man may be a police officer, when he is at home he is a beloved father to his son. But if he comes home firing his revolver, the son will be so frightened that he will forget that he is his beloved father. Naturally, the child loves his father when he's at home like a father, and similarly we love Kṛṣṇa as He is in His eternal abode, in the form of Śyāmasundara.

The *viśva-rūpa* was shown to Arjuna to warn those rascals who claim, "I am God." Arjuna asked to see the *viśva-rūpa* so that in the future we may have some criterion by which to test rascals who claim to be God. In other words, if someone says, "I am God," we can simply reply, "If you are God, please show me your *viśva-rūpa.*" And we can rest assured that such rascals cannot display this form.

Of course, Arjuna was offering all respects to the *viśva-rūpa* form. That is a natural quality of a devotee. A devotee even respects Durgā, Māyā, because Māyā is Kṛṣṇa's energy. If we respect Kṛṣṇa, we respect everyone, even an ant. Therefore Brahmā prays,

sṛṣṭi-sthiti-pralaya-sādhana-śaktir ekā
chāyeva yasya bhuvanāni bibharti durgā
icchānurūpam api yasya ca ceṣṭate sā
govindam ādi-puruṣaṁ tam ahaṁ bhajāmi

"The external potency, Māyā, who is of the nature of the shadow of the *cit* [spiritual] potency, is worshipped by all people as Durgā, the creating, preserving, and destroying agency of this mundane world. I worship the primeval Lord, Govinda, in accordance with whose will Durgā conducts herself." (*Brahma-saṁhitā* 5.44) Thus when we pray to Kṛṣṇa, we pray to Durgā immediately, because Durgā is His energy. And when we pray to Durgā, we are actually praying to Kṛṣṇa, because she is working under the direction of Kṛṣṇa. When the devotee sees the activities of Māyā, he sees Kṛṣṇa immediately, thinking, "Oh, Māyā is acting so nicely under the direction of Kṛṣṇa." When one offers respect to a policeman, he is actually offering respect to the government. Durgā, the material energy, is so powerful that she can create, annihilate, and maintain, but in all cases she is acting under Kṛṣṇa's directions.

Through *bhakti,* pure devotion to Kṛṣṇa, we can leave the association of Māyā and be promoted to the eternal association of Kṛṣṇa. Some of the *gopas,* Kṛṣṇa's friends, are eternal associates, and others are promoted to that eternal position. If only the eternal associates of Kṛṣṇa can play with

Him and others cannot, then what is the meaning of becoming Kṛṣṇa conscious? We can also become eternal associates of Kṛṣṇa through pious deeds executed in many, many lives. Actually, in the Vṛndāvana manifest in this material world, the associates of Kṛṣṇa are mainly conditioned living entities who have been promoted to the perfect stage of Kṛṣṇa consciousness. Thus promoted, they are first of all allowed to see Kṛṣṇa on the planet where Kṛṣṇa's pastimes are being enacted. After this, they are promoted to the transcendental Goloka Vṛndāvana in the spiritual sky. Therefore it is stated in the *Bhāgavatam* (10.12.11), *kṛta-puṇya-puñjāḥ.*

Bhakti-yoga means connecting ourselves with Kṛṣṇa, God, and becoming His eternal associates. *Bhakti-yoga* cannot be applied to any other objective; therefore in Buddhism, for instance, there is no *bhakti-yoga,* because they do not recognise the Supreme Lord existing as the supreme objective. Christians, however, practise *bhakti-yoga* when they worship Jesus Christ, because they are accepting him as the son of God and are therefore accepting God. Unless one accepts God, there is no question of *bhakti-yoga.* Christianity, therefore, is also a form of Vaiṣṇavism, because God is recognised. Nonetheless, there are different stages of God realisation. Mainly, Christianity says, "God is great," and that is a very good assertion, but the actual greatness of God can be understood from *Bhagavad-gītā* and *Śrīmad-Bhāgavatam.* Accepting the greatness of God is the beginning of *bhakti. Bhakti-yoga* also exists among the Muhammadans, because God is the target in the Muslim religion. However, where there is no recognition of a personal God — in other words, where there is only impersonalism — there is no question of *bhakti-yoga. Bhakti-yoga* must include three items: the servitor, the served, and service. One must be present to accept service, and one must be present to render service. The via media is the process of service itself, *bhakti-yoga.* Now, if there is no one to accept that service, how is *bhakti-yoga* possible? Therefore, if a philosophy or religion does not accept God as the Supreme Person, there is no possibility of *bhakti-yoga* being applied.

In the *bhakti-yoga* process, the role of the spiritual master is most important and essential. Although the spiritual master will always come back until his devotees have achieved God realisation, one should not try to take advantage of this. We should not trouble our spiritual master but should complete the *bhakti-yoga* process in this life. The disciple should be serious in his service to the spiritual master, and if the devotee is intelligent, he should think, "Why should I act in such a way that my spiritual master has to take the trouble to reclaim me again? Let me realise Kṛṣṇa in this life." That is the proper way of thinking. We should not think, "Oh, I am sure that my spiritual master will come and save me. Therefore I will do as I please." If we have any affection for our spiritual master, we should complete the process in this life, so that he does not have to return to reclaim us.

In this regard, there is the example of Bilvamaṅgala Ṭhākura, who, in his previous life, was elevated almost to *prema-bhakti,* the highest platform of devotional service. However, since there is always a chance for a falldown, somehow or other he fell down. In his next life, he was born in a very rich *brāhmaṇa* family, in accordance with the principle enunciated in the Sixth Chapter of *Bhagavad-gītā* (6.41): *śucīnāṁ śrīmatāṁ gehe.* Unfortunately, as is often the case with rich boys, he became a prostitute hunter. Yet it is said that his spiritual master instructed him through his prostitute, saying, "Oh, you are so attached to this mere flesh and bones. If you were this much attached to Kṛṣṇa, how much good you might achieve!" Immediately Bilvamaṅgala Ṭhākura resumed his devotional service.

Although the spiritual master assumes responsibility for

his disciple, we should not take advantage of this. Rather, we should try to please the spiritual master (*yasya prasādād bhagavat-prasādaḥ*). We should not put our spiritual master in such a position that he has to reclaim us from a house of prostitution. But even if he has to do so, he will do it, because he assumes this responsibility when he accepts his disciple.

The *bhakti-yoga* process should be completed in this life, because in this life we have all the instruments necessary to become fully Kṛṣṇa conscious. We have *mṛdaṅgas* and cymbals and tongues with which to chant Hare Kṛṣṇa. Even if we don't have *mṛdaṅgas* and cymbals, we have a tongue. No one has to purchase a tongue. We also have ears with which to hear the sound that the tongue vibrates. Therefore we have all the instruments we need with us — a tongue and ears. We have only to chant Hare Kṛṣṇa and use our ears to hear this vibration, and all perfection will be there. We don't have to become highly educated scientists or philosophers. We have only to chant and hear.

Thus we have everything complete. *Pūrṇam adaḥ pūrṇam idam:* everything created by God is complete. This aggregate earth, for instance, is complete. There is sufficient water in the oceans, and the sun acts to evaporate this water, turn it into clouds, and drop rain on the land to produce plants. And from the mountains, pure rivers are flowing to supply water throughout the year. If we want to evaporate a few hundred gallons of water, we have to make many arrangements, but the creation is so complete that millions of tons of water are being drawn from the ocean, turned into clouds, and then sprayed all over the land and reserved on the peaks of mountains so that water will be present for the production of grains and vegetables. Thus the creation is complete because it comes from the complete, and similarly our bodies are also complete for spiritual realisation. The complete machine is already with us. We have only to utilise it to vibrate the transcendental sound (*śabda*) of Hare Kṛṣṇa, and we will attain complete liberation from all material pangs.

CHAPTER NINE

Destination After Death

sarva-dvārāṇi saṁyamya
mano hṛdi nirudhya ca
mūrdhny ādhāyātmanaḥ prāṇam
āsthito yoga-dhāraṇām

"The yogic situation is that of detachment from all sensual engagements. Closing all the doors of the senses and fixing the mind on the heart and the life air at the top of the head, one establishes himself in *yoga*.." (Bg. 8.12)

One translation of the word *yoga* is "plus" — that is, just the opposite of minus. At the present moment, due to our materially contaminated consciousness, we are minus God. When we add God to our lives, when we connect with Him, life is perfected. This process has to be finished at the time of death; therefore as long as we are alive, we have to practise approaching that point of perfection so that at the time of death, when we give up this material body, we can realise the Supreme.

prayāṇa-kāle manasācalena
bhaktyā yukto yoga-balena caiva
bhruvor madhye prāṇam āveśya samyak
sa taṁ paraṁ puruṣam upaiti divyam

"One who, at the time of death, fixes his life air between the eyebrows and by the strength of *yoga*, with an undeviating mind, engages himself in remembering the Supreme Lord in full devotion, will certainly attain to the Supreme Personality of Godhead." (Bg. 8.10) The words *prayāṇa-kāle* mean "at the time of death". Life is kind of a preparation for the final examination, which is death. If we pass that examination, we are transferred to the spiritual world. According to a very common Bengali proverb, "Whatever you do for perfection will be tested at the time of your death."

This process by which the *yogī* closes the doors of the senses is technically called *pratyāhāra,* meaning "just the opposite". Presently, our senses are engaged in seeing worldly beauty. "Just the opposite" means retracting the senses from that beauty and seeing the beauty inside. Hearing is concentrated on the *oṁkāra* sound that is within. Similarly, all the other senses are withdrawn from external activity. The mind is then concentrated on the *viṣṇu-mūrti* within the heart (*manaḥ hṛdi nirudhya*). The word *nirudhya* means "confining" the mind within the heart. When the *yogī* has thus withdrawn his senses and concentrated his mind, he transfers the life air to the top of the head and decides where he should go. There are innumerable planets, and beyond these planets is the spiritual world. The *yogīs* obtain information of these planets from the Vedic literatures, just as, before going to the United States, I obtained information about that country from books. Since all the higher planets in the spiritual world are described in the Vedic literatures, the *yogī* knows everything and can transfer himself to any planet he likes. He does not need a material spaceship.

Scientists have been trying for many years to reach other planets with spaceships, but this is not the process. Maybe by this means one or two men can reach a planet, but that is not the general process. It is not possible for everyone. Generally, if one wants to transfer himself to a higher planet, he practises this *jñāna-yoga* system. Not the *bhakti-yoga* system. The system of *bhakti-yoga* is not used for attaining any material planet.

The devotees of Kṛṣṇa are not interested in any planet within this material universe, because they know that on all planets the four basic miseries exist — birth, old age, disease and death. In the higher planets, one's life span may be much greater than on this earth, but death is ultimately there. Therefore those who are in Kṛṣṇa consciousness are not interested in material life but spiritual life, which means relief from these fourfold miseries. Those who are intelligent do not try to elevate themselves to any planet within this material world. To attain a higher planet, one has to prepare a particular type of body to enable one to live on that planet. We cannot attain these planets by artificial, materialistic means, because a suitable body is necessary to live there. We can stay within water only a short while, but fish are living there their entire lives. But the fish does not have a body suitable for living on the land. Similarly, to enter a higher planet, one has to prepare a suitable body.

In the higher planets, six of our months are equal to one of their days, and the inhabitants of these planets live ten thousand years. This is all described in the Vedic literatures. Although the life span on these planets is very long, there is ultimately death. After ten thousand years, twenty thousand years, or millions of years — it doesn't matter — death is ultimately there.

In the very beginning of *Bhagavad-gītā,* however, we learn that we are not subject to death.

na jāyate mriyate vā kadācin
nāyaṁ bhūtvā bhavitā vā na bhūyaḥ
ajo nityaḥ śāśvato 'yaṁ purāṇo
na hanyate hanyamāne śarīre

"For the soul there is neither birth nor death at any time. He has not come into being, does not come into being, and will not come into being. He is unborn, eternal, ever-existing, undying and primeval. He is not slain when the body is slain." (Bg. 2.20) Kṛṣṇa thus instructs us that we are spirit soul and eternal; therefore why should we subject ourselves to birth and death? One who utilises his intelligence can understand this. One who is situated in Kṛṣṇa consciousness is not interested in promotion to any planet where death exists; rather, being promoted to the spiritual sky, he receives a body just like God's. *Īśvaraḥ paramaḥ kṛṣṇaḥ sac-cid-ānanda-vigrahaḥ.* God's body is *sac-cid-ānanda* — eternal, full of knowledge and full of pleasure. Therefore Kṛṣṇa is called the reservoir of all pleasure. If, upon leaving this body, we transfer ourselves to the spiritual world — to Kṛṣṇa's planet or any other spiritual planet — we attain a similar body full of *sac-cid-ānanda.*

The spirit soul is a very minute particle within the body. It cannot be seen like the external body, but it is sustaining the external body. The object of the *ṣaṭ-cakra* system is to locate the soul at the topmost part of the head. From there, one who is perfect in *dhyāna-yoga* can transfer himself to a higher planet at will. That is the perfection of this type of *yoga.* The *dhyāna-yogī* is somewhat like a traveller who thinks, "Oh, let me see what the moon is like, then I will transfer myself to higher planets." He goes from here to there in the universe, just as on earth travellers go from London to California or Canada. But a Kṛṣṇa conscious person is not interested in such interplanetary travel within the material universe. His goal is service to Kṛṣṇa and transferral to the spiritual sky.

oṁ ity ekākṣaraṁ brahma
vyāharan mām anusmaran

yaḥ prayāti tyajan dehaṁ
sa yāti paramāṁ gatim

"After being situated in this *yoga* practice and vibrating the sacred syllable *oṁ*, the supreme combination of letters, if one thinks of the Supreme Personality of Godhead and quits his body, he will certainly reach the spiritual planets." (Bg. 8.13) *Oṁ*, or *oṁkāra*, is the concise form, or impersonal form, of the transcendental vibration. The *dhyāna-yogī* should vibrate *oṁ* while remembering Kṛṣṇa, or Viṣṇu, the Supreme Personality of Godhead. The impersonal sound of Kṛṣṇa is *oṁ*, but the sound *Hare Kṛṣṇa* contains *oṁ*. Whatever the case, the entire *yoga* system aims at concentration on Viṣṇu. Impersonalists may imagine a form of Viṣṇu, but the personalists do not imagine; they actually *see* the form of the Supreme Lord. Whether one imagines or factually sees, one has to concentrate his mind on the Viṣṇu form. Here the word *mām* means "unto the Supreme Lord, Viṣṇu". If one can remember Viṣṇu upon quitting this body, he can enter into the spiritual kingdom.

One who is intelligent naturally thinks, "I am permanent and eternal. Why should I be interested in things that are not permanent?" Actually, no one wants an existence that is temporary. If we are living in a flat and the landlord asks us to vacate, we have to do so, whether we want to leave or not. However, if we move to a better flat, we are not sorry. It is our nature, however, to want to remain wherever we live. That is because we are permanent and want a permanent residence. Our inclination is to remain. Therefore we don't want to die. We don't want the miseries of birth, old age, disease and death. These are external miseries inflicted by material nature, and they attack us like some fever. In order to extricate ourselves, we have to take certain precautions. To get rid of these miseries, it is necessary to get rid of the material body, because these miseries are inherent in material existence.

Thus by vibrating *oṁ* and leaving the material body thinking of the Supreme Lord, the *yogī* is transferred to the spiritual world. Those who are not personalists, however, cannot enter into the spiritual planet of Lord Śrī Kṛṣṇa. They remain outside, in the *brahmajyoti* effulgence. Just as the sunshine is not different from the sun globe, the *brahmajyoti* effulgence of the Supreme Lord is not different from the Supreme Lord. The impersonalists are placed in that *brahmajyoti* as minute particles. We are all spiritual sparks, and the *brahmajyoti* is full of these spiritual sparks. In this way, the impersonalists merge into the spiritual existence; however, individuality is retained, because the spirit soul is constitutionally an individual. Because the impersonalists don't want a personal form, they are placed and held in the impersonal *brahmajyoti.* There they exist just as atoms exist within the sunshine. The individual spiritual spark remains within the *brahmajyoti* as if homogeneous.

As living entities, we all want enjoyment. We do not simply want existence. We are constitutionally *sac-cid-ānanda* —eternal (*sat*), full of knowledge (*cit*) and full of bliss (*ānanda*). Those who enter the impersonal *brahmajyoti* cannot remain there eternally with the knowledge that "Now I am merged. I am now one with Brahman." Although there is eternality and knowledge, bliss (*ānanda*) is lacking. Who can remain alone in a room year after year reading some book and trying to enjoy himself? We cannot remain alone forever. Eventually we will leave that room and look for some association. It is our nature to want some recreation with others. The impersonalists, dissatisfied with the loneliness of their position in the impersonal effulgence of the

Lord, therefore return again to this material world. This is stated in *Śrīmad-Bhāgavatam* (10.2.32):

ye 'nye 'ravindākṣa vimukta-māninas
tvayy asta-bhāvād aviśuddha-buddhayaḥ
āruhya kṛcchreṇa paraṁ padaṁ tataḥ
patanty adho 'nādṛta-yuṣmad-aṅghrayaḥ

"O lotus-eyed Lord, although nondevotees who accept severe austerities and penances to achieve the highest position may think themselves liberated, their intelligence is impure. They fall down from their position of imagined superiority because they have no regard for Your lotus feet."

The impersonalists are like some astronauts in search of a planet. If they cannot rest in some planet, they have to return to earth. It is herein stated in *Śrīmad-Bhāgavatam* (*anādṛta-yuṣmad-aṅghrayaḥ*) that the impersonalist must return to the material world because he has neglected to serve the Supreme Lord with love and devotion. As long as we are on this earth, we should practise to love and serve Kṛṣṇa, the Supreme Lord; then we can enter His spiritual planet. If we are not trained up in this way, we can enter the *brahmajyoti* as an impersonalist, but there is every risk that we will again fall down into material existence. Out of loneliness, we will search out some association and therefore return to the material world. What we actually want is the eternal association of the Supreme Lord. This is our constitutional position of eternality, knowledge and pleasure. If we are alone, if we do not associate with the Supreme Lord, that pleasure is lacking. For want of pleasure, we feel uncomfortable. For want of pleasure, we will accept any kind of association, any kind of pleasure. Therefore, out of a kind of desperation, we will say, "All right, then let me have material pleasure again." That is the risk the impersonalists take.

In the material world, the highest pleasure is found in sex. That is but a perverted reflection of the pleasure experienced with Kṛṣṇa in the spiritual world. Unless there is sex present in the spiritual world, it cannot be reflected here. However, we should understand that here the reflection is perverted. Actual life is there in Kṛṣṇa. Kṛṣṇa is full of pleasure, and if we train ourselves to serve Him in Kṛṣṇa consciousness, it will be possible at the time of death to transfer ourselves to the spiritual world and enter into Kṛṣṇaloka, Kṛṣṇa's planet, and enjoy ourselves in the association of Kṛṣṇa, the reservoir of all pleasure.

Kṛṣṇa's planet is described in *Brahma-saṁhitā* (5.29) in this way:

cintāmaṇi-prakara-sadmasu kalpa-vṛkṣa-
lakṣāvṛteṣu surabhīr abhipālayantam
lakṣmī-sahasra-śata-sambhrama-sevyamānaṁ
govindam ādi-puruṣaṁ tam ahaṁ bhajāmi

"I worship Govinda, the primeval Lord, the first progenitor, who is tending the *surabhi* cows that fulfil all desires, who is surrounded by millions of purpose (wish-fulfilling) trees and abodes built with spiritual gems, and who is always served with great reverence and affection by hundreds and thousands of goddesses of fortune." In this way Kṛṣṇaloka is described. There the houses are made of touchstone (*cintāmaṇi*). If a small particle of touchstone touches an iron rod, that rod will immediately turn to gold. Of course, in this material world we have no experience with such a thing as touchstone, but according to the *Brahma-saṁhitā* all the abodes in Kṛṣṇaloka are composed of touchstone. Similarly, the trees there are called desire trees (*kalpa-vṛkṣa*) because one can get whatever he desires from them. Here we can get only mangos from a mango tree, but in Kṛṣṇaloka we can get whatever we desire from any tree because the trees are *kalpa-vṛkṣa.* This is just a partial description of Kṛṣṇaloka, Kṛṣṇa's eternal abode in the spiritual sky.

The conclusion, therefore, is not to try to elevate ourselves to any material planet, because the same miserable conditions of birth, old age, disease and death exist in all of them. Scientists are very proud of "scientific" advancement, but they have not been able to check old age, disease and death. They can manufacture something to accelerate death, but nothing that can stop death. That is not within their power.

Those who are intelligent are interested in putting an end to birth, old age, disease and death and entering into a spiritual life full of eternality, bliss and knowledge. The *bhakti-yogī* knows that such a life is possible through practise of Kṛṣṇa consciousness and remembrance of Kṛṣṇa at the time of death.

ananya-cetāḥ satataṁ
yo māṁ smarati nityaśaḥ
tasyāhaṁ sulabhaḥ pārtha
nitya-yuktasya yoginaḥ

"For one who always remembers Me without deviation, I am easy to obtain, O son of Pṛthā, because of his constant engagement in devotional service." (Bg. 8.14) In this verse, the word *nitya-yukta* means "continuously in trance". Such a person who is continuously thinking of Kṛṣṇa and always engaged in Kṛṣṇa consciousness is the highest *yogī.* His attention is not diverted to *jñāna-yoga, dhyāna-yoga* or any other system. For him, there is only one system — Kṛṣṇa. *Ananya-cetāḥ* means "without deviation". A Kṛṣṇa conscious devotee is not disturbed by anything, because his mind is always concentrated on Kṛṣṇa. The word *satatam* means that he is thinking of Kṛṣṇa at all places and at all times. When Kṛṣṇa descended onto this earth, He appeared in Vṛndāvana. Although I may be living in London, my residence is in Vṛndāvana because I am always thinking of Kṛṣṇa. Although I may be in a London flat, my consciousness is there, and this is as good as being there.

Kṛṣṇa consciousness means always living with Kṛṣṇa in His spiritual planet. Because we are conscious of Kṛṣṇa, we are already living with Him. We simply have to wait to give up this material body to go there. For one who remembers Kṛṣṇa without deviation, He is easy to obtain. *Tasyāhaṁ sulabhaḥ pārtha:* "I become very cheap for them." For one who takes to Kṛṣṇa consciousness, the most valuable thing becomes very easy to obtain. Because one is engaged in *bhakti-yoga,* Kṛṣṇa becomes easily available. Why should we try so hard to attain Kṛṣṇa, when Kṛṣṇa Himself says, "I am easy to obtain"? We have only to chant Hare Kṛṣṇa, Hare Kṛṣṇa, Kṛṣṇa Kṛṣṇa, Hare Hare/ Hare Rāma, Hare Rāma, Rāma Rāma, Hare Hare twenty-four hours daily. There is no fast rule and regulation. We can chant in the street or on the tube, in our home or in our office. There is neither expenditure nor tax.

Actually Kṛṣṇa, being omnipotent, is unconquerable, but it is said that He is not only obtained but conquered through pure devotional service. As stated before, it is generally very difficult to realise the Supreme Personality of Godhead; therefore one of His names is Ajita, meaning, "He whom no one can conquer". In *Śrīmad-Bhāgavatam* (10.14.3), Lord Brahmā prays to Ajita,

jñāne prayāsam udapāsya namanta eva
jīvanti san-mukharitāṁ bhavadīya-vārtām

sthāne sthitāḥ śruti-gatāṁ tanu-vāṅ-manobhir
ye prāyaśo 'jita jito 'py asi tais tri-lokyām

"O my dear Lord Ajita, those devotees who have thrown away the impersonal conceptions of the Absolute Truth and have therefore abandoned discussing empiric philosophical truths should hear from self-realised devotees about Your holy name, form, pastimes and qualities. They should completely follow the principles of devotional service and remain free from illicit sex, gambling, intoxication and animal slaughter. Surrendering themselves fully with body, words and mind, they can live in any *āśrama* or social status. Indeed, You are conquered by such persons, although You are always unconquerable."

In this verse, the words *jñāne prayāsam* refer to theosophists and philosophers who are trying year after year and life after life to understand God, or the Absolute Truth. Their attempts are like those of the frog in a well trying to comprehend the vastness of the Atlantic and Pacific oceans. Even our attempts to measure outer space are futile, to say nothing of the attempt to measure God. Such attempts are doomed to failure; therefore *Śrīmad-Bhāgavatam* recommends that we abandon all attempts to measure the Supreme. It is completely useless to try to understand God by our limited knowledge, and an intelligent man understands this. We should become submissive and try to understand that our position is that of a very insignificant segment in this creation. The words *namanta eva* indicate that we are just to become submissive in order to understand the Supreme from a reliable source. And what is that source? *San-mukharitām:* from the lips of realised souls. Arjuna is understanding God directly from the lips of Kṛṣṇa, and we have to understand God through the lips of Arjuna or his bona fide representative. We can understand the transcendental nature of God only from a reliable source. That source may be British, Indian, European, American, Japanese, Hindu, Muslim or whatever. The circumstances are not important. We just have to try to understand by hearing and then try to put the process to practise in our daily lives. By becoming submissive, hearing from the right source and trying to apply the teachings in our daily lives, we can become conquerors of the Supreme. For one who does this, Lord Kṛṣṇa becomes easily available. Ordinarily, God realisation is very difficult, but it is very easy for one who submissively hears (*śruti-gatām*).

There are two processes by which we can acquire knowledge: one is the ascending process (*āroha-panthā*), and the other is the descending process (*avaroha-panthā*). By the ascending process, one attempts to understand God by his own efforts — by philosophising, meditating or speculating. According to the descending process, one acquires knowledge simply by hearing from an authority, from the bona fide spiritual master and the scriptures. As far as the ascending process is concerned, it is stated in *Brahma-saṁhitā* (5.34),

panthās tu koṭi-śata-vatsara-sampragamyo
vāyor athāpi manaso muni-puṅgavānām
so 'py asti yat-prapada-sīmny avicintya-tattve
govindam ādi-puruṣaṁ tam ahaṁ bhajāmi

"I worship Govinda, the primeval Lord, only the tips of the toes of whose lotus feet are approached by the *yogīs* and *jñānis,* who travel for billions of years at the speed of the wind or mind." We can all understand how great the speed of mind is. Although sitting in London, I can immediately think of India, which is thousands and thousands of miles away. It is herein stated that even if one travels at this speed for billions of years, Kṛṣṇa will still remain inconceivable. The word *muni-puṅgavānām* refers to a great thinker, not an ordinary man. Even if such a great thinker travels for millions of years at the speed of mind, he will still find the Supreme Person unknowable. Yet for one who takes undeviatingly to this path of Kṛṣṇa consciousness, Kṛṣṇa is easy to obtain. Why is this? *Nitya-yuktasya yoginaḥ:* "Because such a person is constantly engaged in My devotional service, and I cannot forget him." So this is the process. We have only to become submissive to attract the attention of God. My Guru Mahārāja used to say, "Don't try to see God, but work in such a way that God will see you. God will take care of you. You don't have to *try* to see Him."

This should be our attitude. We should not think, "I want to see God. O God, please come and stand before me. Be like my servant." But since God is no one's servant, we have to oblige Him by our love and service. We all know how difficult it is to see the king or prime minister of a country. It is practically impossible for an ordinary man to get an interview with such an important person, to say nothing of having this important person come and stand before him. Yet people are demanding that the Supreme Personality of Godhead come and stand before them. It is our nature to hanker after Kṛṣṇa, because He is the most attractive, most beautiful, most opulent, most powerful, most learned, and most famous person in the universe. Everyone hankers after these qualities, and Kṛṣṇa is the reservoir of all these qualities, and He possesses them in full. Kṛṣṇa is the reservoir of everything (*raso vai saḥ*); therefore when we hanker after beauty or power or knowledge or fame, we should just turn our attention to Kṛṣṇa. Then we will automatically get whatever our hearts desire.

CHAPTER TEN

The Path of Perfection

mām upetya punar janma
duḥkhālayam aśāśvatam
nāpnuvanti mahātmānaḥ
saṁsiddhiṁ paramāṁ gatāḥ

"After attaining Me, the great souls, who are *yogīs* in devotion, never return to this temporary world, which is full of miseries, because they have attained the highest perfection." (Bg. 8.15)

This material world is certified by its very creator, the Supreme Lord, as *duḥkhālayam,* which means "the place of miseries". Since this is the case, how can we possibly make it comfortable by so-called scientific advancement? *Duḥkha* means "misery" or "suffering", and real suffering is birth, old age, disease and death. We have set these problems aside because we cannot solve them; therefore scientists concentrate on atomic bombs and spaceships. Why can't they solve these important problems that are always causing us to suffer? Obviously, they haven't the power to do so.

But in this verse, Śrī Kṛṣṇa gives the solution: *mām upetya punar janma.* That is, "If one attains My platform, he does not come back again to this place of misery." Unfortunately, in the mode of ignorance, people cannot understand that they are in a miserable situation. Animals cannot understand their miserable situations because they haven't the reason. Man possesses reason whereby he can understand this, but in this age people are using their reasoning power in order to gratify their animal propensities. Reason should be used in getting liberated from this miserable condition. However, if we engage in Kṛṣṇa consciousness twenty-four hours a day without deviation, we will go to Kṛṣṇa and not be reborn in this miserable world. *Mahātmānaḥ saṁsiddhiṁ paramāṁ gatāḥ:* those great souls who have attained the highest perfection, Kṛṣṇa consciousness, are forever freed from misery. In this verse, the word *mahātmā* refers to a Kṛṣṇa conscious man eligible to enter the abode of Kṛṣṇa. The word *mahātmā* does not refer to a political leader like Mahatma Gandhi but to a great soul, a pure devotee of Kṛṣṇa.

When Kṛṣṇa says that the *mahātmā* enters His abode, He is referring to His transcendental kingdom, Goloka Vṛndāvana. The Vṛndāvana from which I have come is called Bhauma Vṛndāvana, which means that it is the same Vṛndāvana descended on this earth. Just as Kṛṣṇa descended on this earth through His own internal potency, similarly His *dhāma,* His abode, also descends. In other words, when Kṛṣṇa descends on this earth, He manifests Himself in that particular land, Vṛndāvana, and therefore that land is also sacred. Apart from this, Kṛṣṇa has His own abode in the spiritual sky, and this is called Goloka Vṛndāvana.

The *mahātmā* prepares in this life to enter that transcendental abode. The human form of life can utilise nature to its best interest. Animals cannot. These facilities should be utilised in striving to become a *mahātmā* and putting an end to birth in this material world, which is characterised by threefold miseries. The threefold miseries are those that pertain to the mind or the body, natural disturbances and miseries caused by other living entities. Whatever our position in this material world, there is always some kind of misery being inflicted upon us. Śrī Kṛṣṇa frankly says that it is not possible to avoid misery in this material world, because this world is meant for misery. Unless miseries are present, we cannot come to Kṛṣṇa consciousness. Misery serves as an impetus to help elevate us to Kṛṣṇa consciousness. An intelligent person understands that although he does not want misery, miseries are being inflicted upon him by force. No one wants misery, but a person should be intelligent enough to question, "Why are these miseries being forced upon me?" Unfortunately, in modern civilisation, people try to set miseries aside, thinking, "Oh, why suffer? Let me cover my miseries with some intoxication." However, the miseries of life cannot be solved by artificial intoxication. As soon as the intoxication is over, one returns to the same point. The miseries of material existence can be solved only by Kṛṣṇa consciousness. If we always remain in Kṛṣṇa consciousness, we'll be transferred to Kṛṣṇa's planet upon leaving this material body. That is called the highest perfection.

People may enquire, "Well, you say that entering Kṛṣṇa's planet constitutes the highest perfection, but we are interested in going to the moon. Is this not a kind of perfection?" Well, the desire to enter the higher planets is always there in the human mind. In fact, another name for the living entity is *sarva-gata,* which means that he wants to travel everywhere. That is the nature of the living entity. Europeans who have money often go to India, America, or some other country, because they do not like to stagnate in one place. That is our nature, and therefore we are interested in going to the moon or wherever. But according to Kṛṣṇa, even if we attain the higher planets, we are still subject to the material miseries.

ā-brahma-bhuvanāl lokāḥ
punar āvartino 'rjuna
mām upetya tu kaunteya
punar janma na vidyate

"From the highest planet in the material world down to the lowest, all are places of misery wherein repeated birth and death take place. But one who attains to My abode, O son of Kuntī, never takes birth again." (Bg. 8.16)

The universe is divided into fourteen planetary systems (*caturdaśa-bhuvana*) — seven lower and seven higher. The earth is situated in the middle. In this verse, Śrī Kṛṣṇa says, *ā-brahma-bhuvanāl lokāḥ:* even if one enters the highest planet, Brahmaloka, there is still birth and death. The words *punar āvartinaḥ* mean "returning again", or "repetition of birth and death". We are changing bodies just as we change clothes, leaving one body and entering another. All planets are filled with living entities. We shouldn't think that only the earth is inhabited. There are living entities on the higher planets and lower planets as well. From our experience, we can see that no place on earth is vacant of living entities. If we dig into the earth, we find some worms, and if we go into the water we find many aquatics. The air is filled with birds, and if we analyse outer space, we will find many living entities. It is illogical to conclude that there are no living entities on the other planets. To the contrary, they are *full* of living entities.

In any case, Kṛṣṇa says that from the highest planet to the lowest planet, there is repetition of birth and death. Yet again, as in the former verse, He says, *mām upetya:* "If you reach My planet, you don't have to return to this miserable material world." To stress this point, Śrī Kṛṣṇa repeats that upon reaching Goloka Vṛndāvana, His eternal abode, one is liberated from the cycle of birth and death and attains eternal life. It is the duty of human life to understand these problems and attain a blissful, eternal life that is full of knowledge. Unfortunately, people in this age have forgotten the aim of life. Why? *Durāśayā ye bahir-artha-māninaḥ* (*Bhāg.* 7.5.31). People have been trapped by the material glitter —

by skyscrapers, big factories and political activities. People do not stop to consider that however big the skyscraper may be, they will not be allowed to live there indefinitely. We should not spoil our energy, therefore, in building great cities but should employ our energy to elevate ourselves to Kṛṣṇa consciousness. Kṛṣṇa consciousness is not a religious formula or some spiritual recreation but is the most important factor in our lives.

People are interested in attaining higher planets because there one's enjoyment is a thousand times greater and the duration of life much longer.

sahasra-yuga-paryantam
ahar yad brahmaṇo viduḥ
rātriṁ yuga-sahasrāntāṁ
te 'ho-rātra-vido janāḥ
(Bg. 8.17)

The duration of the material universe is limited. It is manifested in cycles of *kalpas.* A *kalpa* is a day of Brahmā, and one day of Brahmā consists of a thousand cycles of four *yugas,* or ages: Satya, Tretā, Dvāpara and Kali. The cycle of Satya is characterised by virtue, wisdom and religion, there being practically no ignorance and vice, and the *yuga* lasts 1,728,000 years. In the Tretā-yuga vice is introduced, and this *yuga* lasts 1,296,000 years. In the Dvāpara-yuga there is an even greater decline in virtue and religion, vice increasing, and this *yuga* lasts 864,000 years. And finally, in Kali-yuga (the *yuga* we have now been experiencing over the past 5,000 years), there is an abundance of strife, ignorance, irreligion and vice, true virtue being practically nonexistent, and this *yuga* lasts 432,000 years. In Kali-yuga vice increases to such a point that at the termination of the *yuga,* the Supreme Lord Himself appears as the Kalki-avatāra, vanquishes the demons, saves His devotees and commences another Satya-yuga. Then the process is set rolling again. These four *yugas* rotating a thousand times comprise one day of Brahmā, the creator god, and the same number comprise one night. Brahmā lives one hundred of such "years" and then dies. These "hundred years" by earth calculations total 311 trillion and 40 million earth years. By these calculations, the life of Brahmā seems fantastic and interminable, but from the viewpoint of eternity, it is as brief as a lightning flash. In the Causal Ocean there are innumerable Brahmās rising and disappearing like bubbles in the Atlantic. Brahmā and his creation are all part of the material universe, and therefore they are in constant flux.

In the material universe, not even Brahmā is free from the process of birth, old age, disease and death. Brahmā, however, is directly engaged in the service of the Supreme Lord in the management of this universe; therefore he at once attains liberation. Elevated *sannyāsīs* are promoted to Brahmā's particular planet, Brahmaloka, which is the highest planet in the material universe and which survives all the heavenly planets in the upper strata of the planetary system, but in due course Brahmā and all inhabitants of Brahmaloka are subject to death, according to the law of material nature. So even if we live millions and trillions of years, we have to die. Death cannot be avoided. Throughout the entire universe the process of creation and annihilation is taking place, as described in the next verse:

avyaktād vyaktayaḥ sarvāḥ
prabhavanty ahar-āgame
rātry-āgame pralīyante
tatraivāvyakta-saṁjñake

"At the beginning of Brahmā's day, all living entities become manifest from the unmanifest state, and thereafter, when the night falls, they are merged into the unmanifest again." (Bg. 8.18)

Unless we go to the spiritual sky, there is no escaping this process of birth and death, creation and annihilation. When Brahmā's days are finished, all these planetary systems are covered by water, and when Brahmā rises again, creation takes place. The word *ahar* means "in the day-time", which is twelve hours of Brahmā's life. During this time this material manifestation — all these planets — are seen, but when night comes they are all merged in water. That is, they are annihilated. The word *rātry-āgame* means "at the fall of night". During this time, all these planets are invisible because they are inundated with water. This flux is the nature of the material world.

bhūta-grāmaḥ sa evāyaṁ
bhūtvā bhūtvā pralīyate
rātry-āgame 'vaśaḥ pārtha
prabhavaty ahar-āgame

"Again and again when Brahmā's day arrives, all living entities come into being, and with the arrival of Brahmā's night they are helplessly annihilated." (Bg. 8.19) Although we do not want devastation, devastation is inevitable. At night, everything is flooded, and when day appears, gradually the waters disappear. For instance, on this one planet, the surface is three-fourths covered with water. Gradually, land is emerging, and the day will come when there will no longer be water but simply land. That is nature's process.

paras tasmāt tu bhāvo 'nyo
'vyakto 'vyaktāt sanātanaḥ
yaḥ sa sarveṣu bhūteṣu
naśyatsu na vinaśyati

"Yet there is another unmanifest nature, which is eternal and is transcendental to this manifested and nonmanifested matter. It is supreme and is never annihilated. When all in this world is annihilated, that part remains as it is." (Bg. 8.20)

We cannot calculate the length and breadth of this universe. There are millions and millions of universes like this within this material world, and above this material world is the spiritual sky, where the planets are all eternal. Life on those planets is also eternal. This material manifestation comprises only one fourth of the entire creation. *Ekāṁśena sthito jagat. Ekāṁśena* means "one fourth". Three fourths of the creation is beyond this material sky, which is covered like a ball. This covering extends millions and millions of miles, and only after penetrating that covering can one enter the spiritual sky. That is open sky, eternal sky. In this verse it is stated, *paras tasmāt tu bhāvo 'nyaḥ:* "Yet there is another nature." The word *bhāva* means another "nature". We have experience only with this material nature, but from *Bhagavad-gītā* we understand that there is a spiritual nature that is transcendental and eternal. We actually belong to that spiritual nature, because we are spirit, but presently we are covered by this material body, and therefore we are a combination of the material and spiritual. Just as we can understand that we are a combination of both natures, we should understand also that there is a spiritual world beyond this material universe. Spiritual nature is called superior, and material nature is called inferior, because without spirit, matter cannot move.

This cannot be understood by experimental knowledge. We may look at millions and millions of stars through telescopes, but we cannot approach what we are seeing. Similarly, our senses are so insufficient that we cannot approach an understanding of the spiritual nature. Being incapable, we should not try to understand God and His kingdom by experimental knowledge. Rather, we have to understand by hearing *Bhagavad-gītā.* There is no other way. If we want to know who our father is, we simply have to believe our mother. We have no other way of knowing except by her. Similarly, in order to understand who God is and what His nature is, we have to accept the information given in *Bhagavad-gītā.* There is no question of experimenting. Once we become advanced in Kṛṣṇa consciousness, we will realise God and His nature. We can come to understand, "Yes, there is God and a spiritual kingdom, and I have to go there. Indeed, I must prepare myself to go there."

The word *vyakta* means "manifest". This material universe that we are seeing (or partially seeing) before us is manifest. At least at night we can see that stars are twinkling and that there are innumerable planets. But beyond this *vyakta* is another nature, called *avyakta,* which is unmanifest. That is the spiritual nature, which is *sanātana,* eternal. This material nature has a beginning and an end, but that spiritual nature has neither beginning nor end. This material sky is within the covering of the *mahat-tattva,* matter. This matter is like a cloud. When there is a storm, it appears that the entire sky is covered with clouds, but actually only an insignificant part of the sky is covered. Because we are very minute, if just a few hundred miles are covered, it appears that the entire sky is covered. As soon as a wind comes and blows the clouds away, we can see the sky once again. Like the clouds, this *mahat-tattva* covering has a beginning and an end. Similarly, the material body, being a part of material nature, has a beginning and an end. The body is born, grows, stays for some time, leaves some by-products, dwindles and then vanishes. Whatever material manifestation we see undergoes these six basic transformations. Whatever exists within material nature will ultimately be vanquished. But herein Kṛṣṇa is telling us that beyond this vanishing, cloudlike material nature, there is a superior nature, which is *sanātana*, eternal. *Yaḥ sa sarveṣu bhūteṣu naśyatsu na vinaśyati.* When this material manifestation is annihilated, that spiritual sky remains. This is called *avyakto 'vyaktāt.*

In the Second Canto of *Śrīmad-Bhāgavatam*, we find a description of the spiritual sky and the people who live there. Its nature and features are also discussed. From this Second Canto we understand that there are spiritual aeroplanes in the spiritual sky, and that the living entities there — who are all liberated — travel like lightning on those planes throughout the spiritual sky. This material world is simply an imitation; whatever we see here is simply a shadow of what exists there. The material world is like a cinema, wherein we see but an imitation or a shadow of the real thing that is existing. This material world is only a shadow. As stated in *Śrīmad-Bhāgavatam* (1.1.1), *yatra tri-sargo 'mṛṣā:* "This illusory material world is a combination of matter." In store windows we often see mannequins, but no sane man thinks that these mannequins are real. He can see that they are imitations. Similarly, whatever we see here may be beautiful, just as a mannequin may be beautiful, but it is simply an imitation of the real beauty found in the spiritual world. As Śrīdhara Svāmī says, *yat satyatayā mithyā sargo 'pi satyavat pratīyate:* the spiritual world is real, and this unreal material manifestation only appears to be real. We must understand that reality will never be vanquished and that in essence reality means eternality. Therefore material pleasure, which is temporary, is not actual; real pleasure exists in Kṛṣṇa. Consequently, those who are after the reality don't participate in this shadow pleasure.

Thus when everything in the material world is annihilated, that spiritual nature remains eternally, and it is the purpose of human life to reach that spiritual sky. Unfortunately, people are not aware of the reality of the spiritual sky.

According to *Śrīmad-Bhāgavatam* (7.5.31), *na te viduḥ svārtha-gatiṁ hi viṣṇum:* people do not know their self-interest. They do not know that human life is meant for understanding spiritual reality and preparing oneself to be transferred to that reality. No one can remain here in this material world. All Vedic literatures instruct us in this way. *Tamasi mā jyotir gama:* "Don't remain in this darkness. Go to the light." According to the Fifteenth Chapter of *Bhagavad-gītā* (15.6),

na tad bhāsayate sūryo
na śaśāṅko na pāvakaḥ
yad gatvā na nivartante
tad dhāma paramaṁ mama

"That supreme abode of Mine is not illumined by the sun or moon, nor by fire or electricity. Those who reach it never return to this material world." This material world is dark by nature, and we are artificially illuminating it with electric lights, fire and so on. In any case, its nature is dark, but the spiritual nature is full of light. When the sun is present, there is no darkness; similarly, every planet in the spiritual sky is self-luminous. Therefore there is no darkness, nor is there need of sun, moon or electricity. The word *sūryo* means "sun", *śaśāṅko* means "moon" and *pāvakaḥ* means "fire" or "electricity". So these are not required in the spiritual sky for illumination. And again, Kṛṣṇa herein says, *yad gatvā na nivartante tad dhāma paramaṁ mama:* "That is My supreme abode, and one who reaches it never returns to this material world." This is stated throughout *Bhagavad-gītā.* Again, in this Eighth Chapter (Bg. 8.21),

avyakto 'kṣara ity uktas
tam āhuḥ paramāṁ gatim
yaṁ prāpya na nivartante
tad dhāma paramaṁ mama

"That which the Vedantists describe as unmanifest and infallible, that which is known as the supreme destination, that place from which, having attained it, one never returns—that is My supreme abode." Again, the word *avyakta*, meaning "unmanifest", is used. The word *akṣara* means "that which is never annihilated", or "that which is infallible". This means that since the supreme abode is eternal, it is not subject to the six transformations mentioned previously.

Because we are presently covered by a dress of material senses, we cannot see the spiritual world, and the spiritual nature is inconceivable for us. Yet we can *feel* that there is something spiritual present. Even a man completely ignorant of the spiritual nature can somehow feel its presence. One need only analyse his body silently: "What am I? Am I this finger? Am I this body? Am I this hair? No, I am not this, and I am not that. I am something other than this body. I am something beyond this body. What is that? That is the spiritual." In this way, we can feel or sense the presence of spirituality within this matter. We can sense the absence of spirit when a body is dead. If we witness someone dying, we can sense that something is leaving the body. Although we do not have the eyes to see it, that something is spirit. Its presence in the body is explained in the very beginning of *Bhagavad-gītā* (2.17):

avināśi tu tad viddhi
yena sarvam idaṁ tatam
vināśam avyayasyāsya
na kaścit kartum arhati

"That which pervades the entire body you should know to be indestructible. No one is able to destroy the imperishable soul."

Spiritual existence is eternal, whereas the body is not. It

is said that the spiritual atmosphere is *avyakta*, unmanifest. How, then, can it be manifest for us? Making the unmanifest manifest is this very process of Kṛṣṇa consciousness. According to *Padma Purāṇa*,

> *ataḥ śrī-kṛṣṇa-nāmādi*
> *na bhaved grāhyam indriyaiḥ*
> *sevonmukhe hi jihvādau*
> *svayam eva sphuraty adaḥ*

"No one can understand Kṛṣṇa as He is by the blunt material senses. But He reveals Himself to the devotees, being pleased with them for their transcendental loving service unto Him." In this verse, the word *indriyaiḥ* means "the senses". We have five senses for gathering knowledge (eyes, ears, nose, tongue and skin), and five senses for working (voice, hands, legs, genitals and anus). These ten senses are under the control of the mind. It is stated in this verse that with these dull material senses, we cannot understand Lord Kṛṣṇa's name, form and so forth. Why is this? Kṛṣṇa is completely spiritual, and He is also absolute. Therefore His name, form, qualities and paraphernalia are also spiritual. Due to material conditioning, or material bondage, we cannot presently understand what is spiritual, but this ignorance can be removed by chanting Hare Kṛṣṇa. If a man is sleeping, he can be awakened by sound vibration. You can call him, "Come on, it's time to get up!" Although the person is unconscious, hearing is so prominent that even a sleeping man can be awakened by sound vibration. Similarly, overpowered by this material conditioning, our spiritual consciousness is presently sleeping, but it can be revived by this transcendental vibration of Hare Kṛṣṇa, Hare Kṛṣṇa, Kṛṣṇa Kṛṣṇa, Hare Hare/ Hare Rāma, Hare Rāma, Rāma Rāma, Hare Hare. As stated before, *Hare* refers to the energy of the Lord, and *Kṛṣṇa* and *Rāma* refer to the Lord Himself. Therefore, when we chant Hare Kṛṣṇa, we are praying, "O Lord, O energy of the Lord, please accept me." We have no other prayer than "Please accept me." Lord Caitanya Mahāprabhu taught us that we should simply cry and pray that the Lord accept us. As Caitanya Mahāprabhu Himself prayed,

ayi nanda-tanuja kiṅkaraṁ
patitaṁ māṁ viṣame bhavāmbudhau
kṛpayā tava pāda-paṅkaja-
sthita-dhūlī-sadṛśaṁ vicintaya

"O Kṛṣṇa, son of Nanda, somehow or other I have fallen into this ocean of nescience and ignorance. Please pick me up and place me as one of the atoms at Your lotus feet." If a man has fallen into the ocean, his only hope for survival is that someone comes to pick him up. He only has to be lifted one inch above the water in order to feel immediate relief. Similarly, as soon as we take to Kṛṣṇa consciousness, we are lifted up, and we feel immediate relief.

We cannot doubt that the transcendental is there. *Bhagavad-gītā* is being spoken by the Supreme Personality of Godhead Himself; therefore we should not doubt His word. The only problem is feeling and understanding what He is telling us. That understanding must be developed gradually, and that knowledge will be revealed by the chanting of Hare Kṛṣṇa. By this simple process, we can come to understand the spiritual kingdom, the self, the material world, God, the nature of our conditioning, liberation from material bondage and everything else. This is called *ceto-darpaṇa-mārjanam,* cleaning the dusty mirror of the impure mind.

Whatever the case, we must have faith in the word of Kṛṣṇa. When we purchase a ticket on British Airways or Air

India, we have faith that that company will take us to our destination. Faith is created because the company is authorised. Our faith should not be blind; therefore we should accept that which is recognised. *Bhagavad-gītā* has been recognised as authorised scripture in India for thousands of years, and even outside India there are many scholars, religionists and philosophers who have accepted *Bhagavad-gītā* as authoritative. It is said that even such a great scientist as Albert Einstein was reading *Bhagavad-gītā* regularly. So we should not doubt *Bhagavad-gītā's* authenticity.

Therefore when Lord Kṛṣṇa says that there is a supreme abode and that we can go there, we should have faith that such an abode exists. Many philosophers think that the spiritual abode is impersonal or void. Impersonalists like the Śaṅkarites and Buddhists generally speak of the void or emptiness, but *Bhagavad-gītā* does not disappoint us in this way. The philosophy of voidism has simply created atheism, because it is the nature of the living entity to want enjoyment. As soon as he thinks that his future is void, he will try to enjoy the variegatedness of this material life. Thus impersonalism leads to armchair philosophical discussions and attachment to material enjoyment. We may enjoy speculating, but no real spiritual benefit can be derived from such speculation.

Bhaktiḥ pareśānubhavo viraktir anyatra ca (*Bhāg.* 11.2.42). Once we have developed the devotional spirit, we will become immediately detached from all kinds of material enjoyment. As soon as a hungry man eats, he feels immediate satisfaction and says, "No, I don't want any more. I am satisfied." This satisfaction is a characteristic of the Kṛṣṇa conscious man.

brahma-bhūtaḥ prasannātmā
na śocati na kāṅkṣati

samaḥ sarveṣu bhūteṣu
mad-bhaktiṁ labhate parām

"One who is thus transcendentally situated at once realises the Supreme Brahman and becomes fully joyful. He never laments or desires to have anything. He is equally disposed to every living entity. In that state he attains pure devotional service unto Me." (Bg. 18.54)

As soon as one is spiritually realised, he feels full satisfaction and no longer hankers after flickering material enjoyment. As stated in the Second Chapter of *Bhagavad-gītā* (2.59),

viṣayā vinivartante
nirāhārasya dehinaḥ
rasa-varjaṁ raso 'py asya
paraṁ dṛṣṭvā nivartate

"The embodied soul may be restricted from sense enjoyment, though the taste for sense objects remains. But, ceasing such engagements, by experiencing a higher taste, he is fixed in consciousness." A doctor may tell a diseased man, "Don't eat this. Don't eat that. Don't have sex. Don't. Don't." In this way, a diseased man is forced to accept so many "don't's", but inside he is thinking, "Oh, if I can just get these things, I'll be happy." The desires remain inside. However, when one is established in Kṛṣṇa consciousness, he is so strong inside that he doesn't experience the desire. Although he's not impotent, he doesn't want sex. He can marry thrice, but still be detached. *Paraṁ dṛṣṭvā nivartate.* When something superior is acquired, one naturally gives up all inferior things. That which is superior is the Supreme Personality of Godhead, and atheism and impersonalism cannot give us this. He is attained only by unalloyed devotion.

puruṣaḥ sa paraḥ pārtha
bhaktyā labhyas tv ananyayā
yasyāntaḥ-sthāni bhūtāni
yena sarvam idaṁ tatam

"The Supreme Personality of Godhead, who is greater than all, is attained by unalloyed devotion. Although He is present in His abode, He is all-pervading, and everything is situated within Him." (Bg. 8.22) The words *puruṣaḥ sa paraḥ* indicate the supreme person who is greater than all others. This is not a void speaking, but a person who has all the characteristics of personality in full. Just as we are talking face to face, when we reach the supreme abode we can talk to God face to face. We can play with Him, eat with Him, and everything else. This state is not acquired by mental speculation but by transcendental loving service (*bhaktyā labhyaḥ*). The words *tv ananyayā* indicate that this *bhakti* must be without adulteration. It must be unalloyed.

Although the Supreme Personality is a person and is present in His abode in the spiritual sky, He is so widespread that everything is within Him. He is both inside and outside. Although God is everywhere, He still has His kingdom, His abode. The sun may pervade the universe with its sunshine, yet the sun itself is a separate entity.

In His supreme abode, the Supreme Lord has no rival. Wherever we may be, we find a predominating personality. In the United Kingdom, the predominating personality is the Prime Minister. However, when the next election comes, the Prime Minister will have so many rivals, but in the spiritual sky the Supreme Lord has no rival. Those who want to become rivals are placed in this material world, under the conditions of material nature. In the spiritual sky there is no rivalry, and all the inhabitants therein are liberated souls. From *Śrīmad-Bhāgavatam* we receive information that their bodily features resemble gods. In some of the spiritual planets, God manifests a two-armed form, and in others He manifests a four-armed form. The living entities of those planets have corresponding features, and one cannot distinguish who is God and who is not. This is called *sārūpya-mukti* liberation, wherein one has the same features as the Lord. There are five kinds of liberation: *sāyujya, sārūpya, sālokya, sārṣṭi* and *sāmīpya. Sāyujya-mukti* means merging into God's impersonal effulgence, the *brahmajyoti.* We have discussed this, and have concluded that the attempt to merge and lose individuality is not desirable and is very risky. *Sārūpya-mukti* means attaining a body exactly like God's. *Sālokya-mukti* means living on the same planet with God. *Sārṣṭi-mukti* means having the opulence of God. For instance, God is very powerful, and we can become powerful like Him. That is called *sārṣṭi. Sāmīpya-mukti* means always remaining with God as one of His associates. For instance, Arjuna is always with Kṛṣṇa as His friend, and this is called *sāmīpya-mukti.* We can attain any one of these five types of liberation, but out of these five, *sāyujya-mukti,* merging into the *brahmajyoti,* is rejected by Vaiṣṇava philosophy. According to the Vaiṣṇava philosophy, we worship God as He is and retain our separate identity eternally in order to serve Him. According to the Māyāvāda philosophy, impersonalism, one tries to lose his individual identity and merge into the existence of the Supreme. That, however, is a suicidal policy and is not recommended by Kṛṣṇa in *Bhagavad-gītā.*

This has also been rejected by Lord Caitanya Mahāprabhu, who advocated worship in separation. As stated before, the pure devotee does not even want liberation; he simply asks to remain Kṛṣṇa's devotee birth after birth. This is Lord Caitanya Mahāprabhu's prayer, and the words "birth after birth" indicate that there is no liberation. This means that the devotee doesn't care whether he is liberated or not. He simply wants to engage in Kṛṣṇa consciousness, to serve the Supreme Lord. Always wanting to engage in God's transcendental loving service is the symptom of pure devotion. Of course, wherever a devotee is, he remains in the spiritual kingdom, even though in the material body. On his part, he does not demand any of the five types of liberation, nor anything for his personal superiority or comfort. But in order to associate with God in the spiritual planets, one must become His pure devotee.

For those who are not pure devotees, Lord Kṛṣṇa explains at what times one should leave the body in order to attain liberation.

yatra kāle tv anāvṛttim
āvṛttiṁ caiva yoginaḥ
prayātā yānti taṁ kālaṁ
vakṣyāmi bharatarṣabha

"O best of the Bhāratas, I shall now explain to you the different times at which, passing away from this world, the *yogī* does or does not come back." (Bg. 8.23) In India, unlike in the West, it is common for astrologers to make minute calculations of the astronomical situation at the moment of one's birth. Indeed, a person's horoscope is read not only when he is born but also when he dies, in order to determine what his situation will be in the next life. All this can be determined by astrological calculation. In this verse, Lord Kṛṣṇa is accepting those astrological principles, confirming that if one leaves his body at a particular time, he may attain liberation. If one dies at one moment, he may be liberated, or if he dies at another moment, he may have to return to the material world. It is all a question of "chance", but that chance someway or other is what one has. For the devotee, however, there is no question of chance. Whatever the astrological situation, the devotee in Kṛṣṇa consciousness is guaranteed liberation. For others, there are chances that if they leave their body at a particular moment, they may attain liberation and enter the spiritual kingdom, or they may be reborn.

agnir jyotir ahaḥ śuklaḥ
ṣaṇ-māsā uttarāyaṇam
tatra prayātā gacchanti
brahma brahma-vido janāḥ

"Those who know the Supreme Brahman attain the Supreme by passing away from the world during the influence of the fiery god, in the light, at an auspicious moment of the day, during the fortnight of the waxing moon, or during the six months when the sun travels in the north." (Bg. 8.24) As we all know, the sun's movements are different: six months it is north of the equator, and six months it is south. The sun is also moving, according to Vedic calculations, and from *Śrīmad-Bhāgavatam* we are informed that the sun is situated at the centre of the universe. Just as all the planets are moving, the sun is also moving at a speed calculated to be sixteen thousand miles per second. If a person dies when the sun is in the northern hemisphere, he can attain liberation. That is not only the verdict of *Bhagavad-gītā*, but also of other scriptures.

dhūmo rātris tathā kṛṣṇaḥ
ṣaṇ-māsā dakṣiṇāyanam
tatra cāndramasaṁ jyotir
yogī prāpya nivartate

"The mystic who passes away from this world during the smoke, the night, the fortnight of the waning moon or in the six months when the sun passes to the south reaches the moon planet but again comes back." (Bg. 8.25) No one can say when he is going to die, and in that sense the moment of one's death is accidental. However, for a devotee in Kṛṣṇa consciousness, there is no question of "accidents".

śukla-kṛṣṇe gatī hy ete
jagataḥ śāśvate mate
ekayā yāty anāvṛttim
anyayāvartate punaḥ

"According to Vedic opinion, there are two ways of passing from this world — one in light and one in darkness. When one passes in light, he does not come back; but when one passes in darkness, he returns." (Bg. 8.26) The same description of departure and return is quoted by Ācārya Baladeva Vidyābhūṣaṇa from the *Chāndogya Upaniṣad.* In such a way, those who are fruitive labourers and philosophical speculators from time immemorial are constantly going and coming. Actually they do not attain ultimate salvation, for they do not surrender to Kṛṣṇa.

naite sṛtī pārtha jānan
yogī muhyati kaścana
tasmāt sarveṣu kāleṣu
yoga-yukto bhavārjuna

"Although devotees know these two paths, O Arjuna, they are never bewildered. Therefore be always fixed in devotion." (Bg. 8.27) Herein the Lord confirms that there is no "chance" for one who practises *bhakti-yoga.* His destination is certain. Whether he dies when the sun is in the northern or southern hemisphere is of no importance. As we have already stated, if one thinks of Kṛṣṇa at the time of death, he will at once be transferred to Kṛṣṇa's abode. Therefore Kṛṣṇa tells Arjuna to always remain in Kṛṣṇa consciousness. This is possible through the chanting of Hare Kṛṣṇa. Since Kṛṣṇa and His spiritual kingdom are nondifferent, being absolute, Kṛṣṇa and His sound vibration are the same. Simply by vibrating Kṛṣṇa's name, we can enjoy Kṛṣṇa's association. If we are walking down the street chanting Hare Kṛṣṇa, Kṛṣṇa is also going with us. If we walk down the street and look up at the sky, we may see that the sun or the moon is accompanying us. I can recall about fifty years ago, when I was a householder, my second son, who was about four years old at the time, was walking with me down the street, and he suddenly asked me, "Father, why is the moon going with us?"

If a material object like the moon has the power to accompany us, we can surely understand that the Supreme Lord, who is all-powerful, can always remain with us. Being omnipotent, He can always keep us company, provided that we are also qualified to keep His company. Pure devotees are always merged in the thought of Kṛṣṇa and are always remembering that Kṛṣṇa is with them. Lord Caitanya Mahāprabhu has confirmed the absolute nature of Kṛṣṇa in His *Śikṣāṣṭaka* (verse 2):

nāmnām akāri bahudhā nija-sarva-śaktis
tatrārpitā niyamitaḥ smaraṇe na kālaḥ
etādṛśī tava kṛpā bhagavan mamāpi
durdaivam īdṛśam ihājani nānurāgaḥ

"My Lord, O Supreme Personality of Godhead, in Your holy name there is all good fortune for the living entity, and therefore You have many names, such as Kṛṣṇa and Govinda, by which You expand Yourself. You have invested all Your potencies in those names, and there are no hard-and-fast rules for remembering them. My dear Lord, although You bestow such mercy upon the fallen, conditioned souls by liberally teaching Your holy names, I am so unfortunate that I commit offences while chanting the holy name, and therefore I do not achieve attachment for chanting."

We may take the effort to spend a great deal of money and attempt to build or establish a temple for Kṛṣṇa, but if we do so we must observe many rules and regulations and see properly to the temple's management. But herein it is confirmed that simply by chanting, any man can have the benefit of keeping company with Kṛṣṇa. Just as Arjuna is deriving benefit by being in the same chariot with Lord Śrī Kṛṣṇa, we can also benefit by associating with Kṛṣṇa through the chanting of His holy names — Hare Kṛṣṇa, Hare Kṛṣṇa, Kṛṣṇa Kṛṣṇa, Hare Hare/ Hare Rāma, Hare Rāma, Rāma Rāma, Hare Hare. This *mahā-mantra* is not my personal concoction but is authorised by Lord Caitanya Mahāprabhu, who is considered to be not only an authority but the incarnation of Lord Śrī Kṛṣṇa Himself. It was Lord Caitanya Mahāprabhu who said, "O Lord, You are so kind to the people of this material world that You expand Yourself in Your holy name so that they can associate with You."

Although the *mahā-mantra* is in the Sanskrit language and many people do not know its meaning, it is still so attractive that people participate when it is chanted publicly. When chanting the *mahā-mantra,* we are completely safe, even in this most dangerous position. We should always be aware that in this material world, we are always in a dangerous position. *Śrīmad-Bhāgavatam* confirms: *padaṁ padaṁ yad vipadāṁ na teṣāṁ.* In this world, there is danger at every step. The devotees of the Lord, however, are not meant to remain in this miserable, dangerous place. Therefore we should take care to advance in Kṛṣṇa consciousness while in this human form. Then our happiness is assured.

Appendixes

The Author

His Divine Grace A.C. Bhaktivedanta Swami Prabhupāda appeared in this world in 1896 in Calcutta, India. He first met his spiritual master, Śrīla Bhaktisiddhānta Sarasvatī Gosvāmī, in Calcutta in 1922. Bhaktisiddhānta Sarasvatī was a prominent religious scholar and the founder of the Gauḍīya Maṭha (a *Vaiṣṇava* movement with sixty-four centres) in India. He liked this educated young man and convinced him to dedicate his life to teaching Vedic knowledge. Śrīla Prabhupāda became his student and, in 1933, received initiation as his disciple.

At their first meeting Śrīla Bhaktisiddhānta Sarasvatī requested Śrīla Prabhupāda to broadcast Vedic knowledge in English. In the years that followed, Śrīla Prabhupāda wrote a commentary on the *Bhagavad-gītā* and assisted the Gauḍīya Maṭha in its work. In 1944, he started *Back to Godhead,* a fortnightly magazine in English. Singlehandedly, Śrīla Prabhupāda edited it, typed the manuscripts, checked the galley proofs, and even distributed the individual copies. The magazine now continues to be published by his disciples throughout the world in different languages.

In 1950 Śrīla Prabhupāda retired from domestic life to devote more time to his studies and writing. He travelled to the holy town of Vṛndāvana, where he lived in humble circumstances in the historic temple of Rādhā-Dāmodara. There, for several years, he engaged in deep study and writing. He accepted the renounced order of life (*sannyāsa*) in 1959. It was at the Rādhā-Dāmodara temple that Śrīla Prabhupāda began to work on his life's masterpiece: a multivolume translation of the eighteen-thousand verse *Śrīmad-Bhāgavatam* (*Bhāgavata Purāṇa*) with full commentary. After publishing three volumes of the *Bhāgavatam*, Śrīla Prabhupāda travelled by freighter to New York City. He was practically penniless, but had faith that the mission of his spiritual master could be successful. On the day he landed in America and saw the grey mists hanging over the towering skyscrapers, he penned these words in his diary: "My dear Lord Kṛṣṇa, I am sure that when this transcendental message penetrates their hearts, they will certainly feel gladdened and thus become liberated from all unhappy conditions of life." He was sixty-nine years old, alone and with few resources, but the wealth of spiritual knowledge and devotion he possessed was an unwavering source of strength and inspiration.

"At a very advanced age, when most people would be resting on their laurels," writes Harvey Cox, Harvard University theologian and author, "Śrīla Prabhupāda harkened to the mandate of his own spiritual teacher and set out on the difficult and demanding voyage to America. Śrīla Prabhupāda is, of course, only one of thousands of teachers. But in another sense, he is one in a thousand, maybe one in a million."

In 1966, Śrīla Prabhupāda founded the International Society for Krishna Consciousness, which became the formal name for the Hare Kṛṣṇa Movement.

In the years that followed, Śrīla Prabhupāda gradually attracted tens of thousands of followers, started more than a hundred temples and *āśramas,* and published scores of books. His achievement is remarkable in that he transplanted India's ancient spiritual culture to the twentieth-century Western world.

In 1968, Śrīla Prabhupāda sent three devotee couples to bring Kṛṣṇa consciousness to the U.K. At first, these devotees were cared for by Hindu families who appreciated their mission, but soon they became well known in London for the street-chanting on Oxford Street. A headline in the *Times* announced, "Kṛṣṇa Chant Startles London". But the *mahā-mantra* soon became popular. Former Beatle, George Harrison, who had known Śrīla Prabhupāda and the chanting before the devotees came to England, wanted to help. He arranged to produce a recording of the *mantra* on the Beatles' Apple label. It reached the Top Ten in Britain and number one in some other countries.

When Śrīla Prabhupāda arrived in England, he was the guest of John Lennon at his estate in Tittenhurst, while work was progressing on the temple in Bloomsbury, near the British Museum. In November 1969, Śrīla Prabhupāda opened the temple — the first Rādhā-Kṛṣṇa temple in Europe. The movement grew from strength to strength. Once again, George Harrison offered to help by donating a beautiful mock-Tudor manor house and estate in Hertfordshire. Now named Bhaktivedanta Manor, it is the Society's main training centre in Britain.

New devotees of Kṛṣṇa soon became highly visible in all the major cities around the world by their public chanting and their distribution of Śrīla Prabhupāda's books of Vedic knowledge. They began staging joyous cultural festivals throughout the year and serving millions of plates of delicious food offered to Kṛṣṇa (known as *prasādam*) throughout the world. As a result, ISKCON has significantly influenced the lives of hundreds of thousands of people. The late A. L. Basham, one of the world's leading authorities on Indian history and culture, wrote, "The Hare Kṛṣṇa movement arose out of next to nothing in less than twenty years and has become known all over the West. This is an important fact in the history of the Western world."

In just twelve years, despite his advanced age, Śrīla Prabhupāda circled the globe fourteen times on lecture tours that took him to six continents. Yet this vigorous schedule did not slow his prolific literary output. His writings constitute a veritable library of Vedic philosophy, religion, literature, and culture.

Indeed, Śrīla Prabhupāda's most significant contribution is his books. Highly respected by academics for their authority, depth and clarity, they are used as textbooks in numerous university courses.

Garry Gelade, a professor at Oxford University's Department of Philosophy, wrote of them: "These texts are to be treasured. No one of whatever faith or philosophical persuasion who reads these books with an open mind can fail to be moved and impressed." And Dr. Larry Shinn, Dean of the College of Arts and Sciences at Bucknell University, wrote, "Prabhupāda's personal piety gave him real authority. He exhibited complete command of the scriptures, and unusual depth of realization, and an outstanding personal example, because he actually lived what he taught."

His writings have been translated into over 50 languages. The Bhaktivedanta Book Trust, established in 1972 to publish the works of Śrīla Prabhupāda, has thus become the world's largest publisher of books in the field of Indian religion and philosophy. 450 million copies in over 50 languages had been sold by the end of 1991.

Before he passed away on the 14th of November 1977 he had guided that Society and seen it grow to a world-wide confederation of more than one hundred *āśramas*, schools, temples, institutes, and farm communities.

References

The text of *The Path of Perfection* is confirmed by standard Vedic authorities. The following authentic scriptures are specifically cited in this volume:

Bhagavad-gītā, 2, 7, 9-10, 14, 15, 16, 20, 24, 28, 29, 29-30, 34, 37, 40, 41, 43, 48, 49, 49-50, 54, 57, 58, 62, 64, 67, 70, 70-71, 72, 73, 74, 74-75, 77, 78-79, 81-82, 85, 86, 87, 90, 90-91, 94, 95-96, 97, 98, 99-100, 101, 104, 105, 106, 106-107, 108, 110-112, 114, 116, 118, 119, 119-120, 121, 125-126, 129-130, 133, 136, 136-137, 138-139, 139-140, 144, 149, 151-152, 153, 154-155, 155, 155-156, 159, 159-160, 160, 163-164, 164, 165, 167, 168, 168-169, 169

Bhāgavata. See: Śrīmad-Bhāgavatam

Brahma-saṁhitā, 12, 32, 32-33, 33, 34-35, 59-60, 60, 89, 94, 95, 131, 143, 147

Bṛhan-nāradīya Purāna, 44

Caitanya-caritāmṛta, 28, 41

Kaṭha Upaniṣad, 77

Nārada-pañcarātra, 99

Padma Purāṇa, 30, 33, 161

Ṣaḍ-gosvāmy-aṣṭaka, 91-92

Śikṣāṣṭaka, 2-3, 126, 129, 170-171

Śrīmad-Bhāgavatam, 25, 26, 38, 39, 45-46, 48, 51, 68, 73, 121-122, 132, 142, 145-146, 152, 158, 163, 171

Stotra-ratna, 73

Upadeśāmṛta, 76, 84

Vedānta-sūtra, 11, 32, 48

Viṣṇu-Purāna, 24

Glossary

A

Arjuna — the intimate friend of Lord Kṛṣṇa who heard *Bhagavad-gītā* from Him on the battlefield of Kurukṣetra.

Āśrama — the four spiritual orders of Vedic society: celibate student, householder, retired, and renounced.

Aṣṭāṅga-yoga — the eight-step process of mystic meditation taught by Patañjali.

Avatāra — a "descent", an appearance of Supreme Lord in this world.

B

Bhagavad-gītā — the discourse between the Supreme Lord, Kṛṣṇa, and His devotee Arjuna expounding devotional service as both the principal means and the ultimate end of spiritual perfection.

Bhakti-yoga — the process of reestablishing one's personal relationship with the Supreme Lord through devotional service.

Brahmacārī — one in the first order of spiritual life, a celibate student.

Brahman — the Absolute Truth; especially the impersonal aspect of the Absolute.

Brāhmaṇa — a member of the intelligent and priestly class.

C

Caitanya Mahāprabhu — Lord Kṛṣṇa Himself, appearing as the special incarnation for this age and the deliverer of the process of chanting the Supreme Lord's holy names.

Causal Ocean — the corner of the spiritual universe in which the Lord in His form as Mahā-Viṣṇu lies down to create the entirety of material universes.

D

Daridra-nārāyaṇa — "poor Nārāyaṇa", a misconception of impersonalists that the common man is equal to God.

Dhyāna-yoga — the process of linking with the Supreme by meditating on the Supersoul in the heart.

Dvāpara-yuga — the third in the cycle of four ages. *See also: Yugas*

G

Goloka Vṛndāvana — the highest spiritual planet, Lord Kṛṣṇa's personal abode.

Gopīs — Kṛṣṇa's cowherd girl friends, His most confidential devotees.

Gosvāmīs, the six — Rūpa, Sanātana, Raghunātha dāsa, Gopāla Bhaṭṭa, Raghunātha Bhaṭṭa, and Jīva Gosvāmīs, immediate followers of Lord Caitanya Mahāprabhu who were empowered by Him to establish the preaching of His movement all over the world.

Govinda — Lord Kṛṣṇa, the giver of pleasure to the cows, the land, and the senses.

Gṛhastha — a householder, member of the second spiritual order of Vedic society.

H

Hari-nāma — the holy name of the Supreme Lord Hari (Kṛṣṇa).

Haṭha-yogas — *See: Aṣṭāṅga-yoga*

J

Jagannātha — the Supreme Lord Viṣṇu appearing in His Deity form in the city of Purī in Orissa. The worshipable Deity of Lord Caitanya Mahāprabhu.

Jñāna-yoga — process of linking with the Supreme by cultivation of knowledge.

Jñānīs — those who practice *jñāna-yoga.*

K

Kali-yuga — the current age of quarrel, begun 5,000 years ago and scheduled to last 427,000 more years.

Karma-yoga — the process of linking with the Supreme by surrendering the results of fruitive work.

Kīrtana — the devotional process of chanting; glorification of the holy names of the Supreme Lord.

Kṛṣṇaloka — *See:* Goloka Vṛndāvana

Kṣatriyas — warriors and administrators, the second occupational order of Vedic society.

M

Mahā-mantra — the great chanting for deliverance:

Hare Kṛṣṇa, Hare Kṛṣṇa, Kṛṣṇa Kṛṣṇa, Hare Hare
Hare Rāma, Hare Rāma, Rāma Rāma, Hare Hare

Mantra — a Vedic sound vibration that can deliver the mind from illusion.

Māyā — the material energy, the Supreme Lord's deluding potency.

Mṛdaṅga — an oblong clay drum used in congregational chanting of the Lord's holy names.

N

Nṛsiṁhadeva — the appearance of Lord Viṣṇu as half-lion, half-man to protect His devotee Prahlāda and kill the demon Hiraṇyakaśipu.

O

Oṁ(kāra) — the sacred seed-syllable in the Vedas which is the compact representation of the Absolute Truth.

P

Prema-bhakti — perfected devotional service on the platform of pure ecstatic love of God.

R

Rādhā — the personal consort of Lord Kṛṣṇa, His internal pleasure potency.

Rāma — the Supreme Lord, the reservoir of all pleasure.

Rāmānujācārya — the great Vaiṣṇava spiritual master who reestablished the ancient line of disciplic succession from the goddess of fortune (Śrī-sampradāya) in this age.

Rasagullās — curd balls boiled in sugar juice.

S

Samosās — deep-fried vegetable pies.

Sāṅkhya-yoga — the process of linking with the Supreme by intellectually tracing out the source of creation.

Saṅkīrtana — *See: Kīrtana*

Sannyāsī — one in the renounced order of life, the highest of the four spiritual divisions of Vedic society.

Śāstras — revealed scriptures.

Satya-yuga — the first and purest in the cycle of four ages. *See also: Yugas*

Śrīmad-Bhāgavatam — the "spotless *Purāṇa,*" which presents the entire science of God consciousness, without any tinge of material religiosity.

Surabhi — the cows of the spiritual world, which can be milked to yield any desire.

Śyāmasundara — the "dark, beautiful boy" of Vṛndāvana, Lord Kṛṣṇa.

T

Tretā-yuga — the second in the cycle of four ages. *See also: Yugas*

V

Vaiṣṇavas — worshipers of the Supreme Lord, Viṣṇu.

Vedas — the original revealed scriptures.

Viṣṇu — the Supreme Lord in His opulent feature as the Lord of Vaikuṇṭha.
Viṣṇu-mūrti — the personal form of Lord Viṣṇu.
Vṛndāvana — the village in which Lord Kṛṣṇa enacts His most intimate pastimes. *See also:* Goloka Vṛndāvana.

Y

Yogī — one who has achieved, or is striving for, union with the Supreme.
Yugas — the four great ages of universal time, which occur in repeated cycles of 4,320,000 years.

Guide to Sanskrit Pronunciation

Throughout the centuries, the Sanskrit language has been written in a variety of alphabets. The mode of writing most widely used throughout India, however, is called *devanāgarī*, which means, literally, the writing used in "the cities of the demigods". The *devanāgarī* alphabet consists of forty-eight characters, including thirteen vowels and thirty-five consonants. Ancient Sanskrit grammarians arranged the alphabet according to practical linguistic principles, and this order has been accepted by all Western scholars. The system of transliteration used in this book conforms to a system that scholars in the last fifty years have accepted to indicate the pronunciation of each Sanskrit sound.

The short vowel **a** is pronounced like the **u** in b**u**t, long **ā** like the **a** in f**a**r, and short **i** like the **i** in p**i**n. Long **ī** is pronounced as in p**i**que, short **u** as in p**u**ll, and long **ū** as in r**u**le. The vowel **ṛ** is pronounced like the **ri** in **ri**m. The vowel **e** is pronounced as in th**ey**, **ai** as in **ai**sle, **o** as in g**o**, and **au** as in h**ow**. The *anusvāra* (**ṁ**), which is a pure nasal, is pronounced like the **n** in the French word *bo***n**, and *visarga* (**ḥ**), which is a strong aspirate, is pronounced as a final **h** sound. Thus **aḥ** is pronounced like **aha**, and **iḥ** like **ihi**.

The guttural consonants — **k, kh, g, gh,** and **ṅ** — are pronounced from the throat in much the same manner as in English. **K** is pronounced as in **k**ite, **kh** as in E**ckh**art, **g** as in **g**ive, **gh** as in di**g h**ard, and **ṅ** as in si**ng**. The palatal consonants — **c, ch, j, jh,** and **ñ** — are pronounced from the palate with the middle of the tongue. **C** is pronounced as in **ch**air, **ch** as in staun**ch-h**eart, **j** as in **j**oy, **jh** as in he**dgeh**og, and **ñ** as in ca**ny**on. The cerebral consonants — **ṭ, ṭh, ḍ, ḍh,** and **ṇ** — are pronounced with the tip of the tongue turned up and drawn back against the dome of the palate. **Ṭ** is pronounced as in tub, **ṭh** as in ligh**t-h**eart, **ḍ** as in **d**ove, **ḍh** as in re**d-h**ot, and **ṇ** as in **n**ut. The dental consonants — **t, th, d, dh,** and **n** — are pronounced in the same manner as the cerebrals, but with the forepart of the tongue against the teeth. The labial consonants — **p, ph, b, bh,** and **m** — are pronounced with the lips. **P** is pronounced as in **p**ine, **ph** as in u**ph**ill, **b** as in **b**ird, **bh** as in ru**b-h**ard, and **m** as in **m**other. The semivowels — **y, r, l,** and **v** — are pronounced as in **y**es, **r**un, **l**ight, and **v**ine respectively. The sibilants **ś, ṣ,** and **s** — are pronounced, respectively, as in the German word **s***prechen* and the English words **sh**ine and **s**un. The letter **h** is pronounced as in **h**ome.

An Introduction to ISKCON and Devotee Life

What is the International Society for Krishna Consciousness?

The International Society for Krishna Consciousness (ISKCON), popularly known as the Hare Kṛṣṇa movement, is a world-wide association of devotees of Kṛṣṇa, the Supreme Personality of Godhead. The same God is known by many names in the various scriptures of the world. In the Bible He is known as Jehovah ("the almighty one"), in the Koran as Allah ("the great one"), and in the *Bhagavad-gītā* as Kṛṣṇa, a Sanskrit name meaning "the all-attractive one".

The movement's main purpose is to promote the well-being of human society by teaching the science of God consciousness (Kṛṣṇa consciousness) according to the timeless Vedic scriptures of India.

The best known of the Vedic texts is the *Bhagavad-gītā* ("Song of God"). It is said to date back 5,000 years to the time when Kṛṣṇa incarnated on earth to teach this sacred message. It is the philosophical basis for the Hare Kṛṣṇa movement and is revered by more than 700 million people today.

This exalted work has been praised by scholars and leaders the world over. M.K. Gandhi said, "When doubts haunt me, when disappointments stare me in the face and I see not one ray of hope, I turn to the *Bhagavad-gītā* and find a verse to comfort me." Ralph Waldo Emerson wrote, "It was the first of books; it was as if an empire spoke to us, nothing small or unworthy, but large, serene, consistent, the voice of an old intelligence which in another age and climate had pondered and thus disposed of the same questions which exercise us." And Henry David Thoreau said, "In the morning I bathe my intellect in the stupendous and cosmogonal philosophy of the *Bhagavad-gītā*."

Lord Kṛṣṇa teaches in the *Bhagavad-gītā* that we are not these temporary material bodies but are spirit souls, or conscious entities, and that we can find genuine peace and happiness only in spiritual devotion to God. The *Gītā* and other world scriptures recommend that people joyfully chant the holy name of God. Whether one chants His name as Kṛṣṇa, Allah, or Jehovah, one may become blessed with pure love of God.

A Sixteenth-Century Incarnation of Kṛṣṇa

Kṛṣṇa incarnated again in the sixteenth century as Śrī Caitanya Mahāprabhu and popularized the chanting of God's names all over India. He constantly sang these names of God, as prescribed in the Vedic literatures: Hare Kṛṣṇa, Hare Kṛṣṇa, Kṛṣṇa Kṛṣṇa, Hare Hare/Hare Rāma, Hare Rāma, Rāma Rāma, Hare Hare. The Hare Kṛṣṇa *mantra* is a transcendental sound vibration. It purifies the mind and awakens the dormant love of God in the hearts of all living beings. Lord Caitanya requested His followers to spread this chanting to every town and village of the world.

Anyone can take part in the chanting of Hare Kṛṣṇa and learn the science of spiritual devotion by studying the *Bhagavad-gītā*. This easy and practical process of self-realization will awaken our natural state of peace and happiness.

Many academics and religious leaders who understand the

roots of the modern day Hare Kṛṣṇa movement have affirmed the movement's authenticity. Diana L. Eck, professor of comparative religion and Indian studies at Harvard University, describes the movement as a "tradition that commands a respected place in the religious life of humankind."

Hare Kṛṣṇa Lifestyles

The devotees seen dancing and chanting in the streets, dressed in traditional Indian robes, are, for the most part, full-time students of the Hare Kṛṣṇa movement. The vast majority of followers, however, live and work in the general community, practising Kṛṣṇa consciousness in their homes and attending temples on a regular basis.

There are about 5,000 full-time devotees throughout the world and 200,000 congregational members outside of India. The movement is presently comprised of 267 temples, 40 rural communities, 26 schools, and 45 restaurants in 71 countries. The basic principle of the Hare Kṛṣṇa lifestyle is "simple living and high thinking". A devotee of Kṛṣṇa is encouraged to use his time, energy, talents, and resources in devotional service to God, and not to hanker for selfish ambitions or pleasures which result in frustration and anxiety.

Devotees try to cultivate humanity's inherent spiritual qualities of compassion, truthfulness, cleanliness and austerity. There are four regulative principles which devotees adopt to assist them to develop those qualities and also to help control the insatiable urges of the mind and senses. These are:

1. No eating of meat, fish or eggs.
2. No gambling.
3. No sex other than for procreation within marriage.
4. No intoxication, including all recreational drugs, alcohol, tobacco, tea and coffee.

According to the *Bhagavad-gītā,* indulgence in the above activities disrupts our physical, mental, and spiritual well-being and increases anxiety and conflict in society.

A Philosophy for Everyone

The philosophy of the Hare Kṛṣṇa movement is a non-sectarian monotheistic tradition. It may be summarized in the following eight points:

1. By sincerely cultivating an authentic spiritual science, we can become free from anxiety and achieve a state of pure, unending, blissful consciousness.
2. Each one of us is not the material body but an eternal spirit soul, part and parcel of God (Kṛṣṇa). As such, we are all interrelated through Kṛṣṇa, our common father.
3. Kṛṣṇa is eternal, all-knowing, omnipresent, all-powerful, and all-attractive. He is the seed-giving father of all living beings and the sustaining energy of the universe. He is the source of all incarnations of God.
4. The *Vedas* are the oldest scriptures in the world. The essence of the *Vedas* is found in the *Bhagavad-gītā,* a literal record of Kṛṣṇa's words spoken 5,000 years ago in India. The goal of Vedic knowledge — and of all theistic religions — is to achieve love of God.
5. We can perfectly understand the knowledge of self-realization through the instructions of a genuine spiritual master — one who is free from selfish motives and whose mind is firmly fixed in meditation on Kṛṣṇa.
6. All that we eat should first be offered to Kṛṣṇa with a prayer. In this way Kṛṣṇa accepts the offering and blesses it for our purification.
7. Rather than living in a self-centred way, we should act for the pleasure of Kṛṣṇa. This is known as *bhakti-yoga,* the science of devotional service.

8. The most effective means for achieving God consciousness in this age is to chant the holy names of the Lord: Hare Kṛṣṇa, Hare Kṛṣṇa, Kṛṣṇa Kṛṣṇa, Hare Hare, Hare Rāma, Hare Rāma, Rāma Rāma, Hare Hare.

Kṛṣṇa Consciousness at Home

From what we've read in this book, it is clear how important it is for everyone to practise Kṛṣṇa consciousness, devotional service to Lord Kṛṣṇa. Of course, living in the association of Kṛṣṇa's devotees in a temple or *aśrama* makes it easier to perform devotional service. But if you're determined, you can follow the teachings of Kṛṣṇa consciousness at home and thus convert your home into a temple.

Spiritual life, like material life, means practical activity. The difference is that, whereas we perform material activities for the benefit of ourselves or those we consider ours, we perform spiritual activities for the benefit of Lord Kṛṣṇa, under the guidance of the scriptures and the spiritual master. Kṛṣṇa declares in the *Bhagavad-gītā* that a person can achieve neither happiness nor the supreme destination of life — going back to Godhead, back to Lord Kṛṣṇa — if he or she does not follow the injunctions of the scriptures. How to follow the scriptural rules by engaging in practical service to the Lord is explained by a bona fide spiritual master who is in an authorized chain of disciplic succession coming from Kṛṣṇa Himself.

The timeless practices that are outlined in this book have been taught to us by His Divine Grace A. C. Bhaktivedanta Swami Prabhupāda, the foremost exponent of Kṛṣṇa consciousness in our time.

The purpose of spiritual knowledge is to bring us closer to God, or Kṛṣṇa. Kṛṣṇa says in the *Bhagavad-gītā* (18.55), *bhaktyā mām abhijānāti:* "I can be known only by devotional service." Spiritual knowledge guides us in proper action to satisfy the desires of Kṛṣṇa through practical engagements in His loving service. Without practical application, theoretical knowledge is of little value.

Spiritual knowledge offers direction in all aspects of life. We should endeavour, therefore, to organize our lives in such a way as to follow Kṛṣṇa's teachings as far as possible. We should try to do our best, to do more than is simply convenient. Then it will be possible for us to rise to the transcendental plane of Kṛṣṇa consciousness, even while living far from a temple.

Chanting Hare Kṛṣṇa

The first principle in devotional service is to chant the Hare Kṛṣṇa *mahā-mantra* (*mahā* means "great"; *mantra* means "sound that liberates the mind from ignorance"):

Hare Kṛṣṇa, Hare Kṛṣṇa, Kṛṣṇa Kṛṣṇa, Hare Hare
Hare Rāma, Hare Rāma, Rāma Rāma, Hare Hare

You can chant these holy names of the Lord anywhere and at any time, but it is best to do it at a specific time of the day. Early morning hours are ideal.

The chanting can be done in two ways: singing the *mantra,* called *kīrtana* (usually done in a group), and saying the *mantra* to oneself, called *japa* (which literally means "to speak softly"). Concentrate on hearing the sound of the holy names. As you chant, pronounce the names clearly and distinctly, addressing Kṛṣṇa in a prayerful mood. When your mind wanders, bring it back to the sound of the Lord's name. Chanting is a prayer to Kṛṣṇa that means "O energy of the Lord (Hare), O all-attractive Lord (Kṛṣṇa), O supreme enjoyer (Rāma), please engage me in Your service." The more attentively and sincerely you chant these names of God, the more spiritual progress you will make.

Because God is all-powerful and all-merciful, He has kindly made it very easy for us to chant His names, and He has also invested all His powers in them. Therefore the names of God and God Himself are identical. This means that when we chant the holy names of Kṛṣṇa and Rāma we are directly associating with God and being purified by such communion. Therefore we should always try to chant with devotion and reverence. The Vedic literature states that Lord Kṛṣṇa is personally dancing on your tongue when you chant His holy name.

When you chant alone, it is best to chant on *japa* beads (available at any of the centres listed in the advertisement at the end of this book). This not only helps you fix your attention on the holy name, but also helps you count the number of times you chant the *mantra* daily. Each strand of *japa* beads contains 108 small beads and one large bead, the head bead. Begin on a bead next to the head bead and gently roll it between the thumb and middle finger of your right hand as you chant the full Hare Kṛṣṇa *mantra.* Then move to the next bead and repeat the process. In this way, chant on each of the 108 beads until you reach the head bead again. This is called one "round" of *japa.* Then, without chanting on the head bead, reverse the beads and start your second round on the last bead you chanted on.

Initiated devotees vow before the spiritual master to chant at least sixteen rounds of the Hare Kṛṣṇa *mantra* daily. But even if you can chant only one round a day, the principle is that once you commit yourself to chanting that round, you should try to complete it every day without fail. When you feel you can chant more, then increase the minimum number of rounds you chant each day — but try not to fall below that number. You can chant more than your fixed number, but you should maintain a set minimum each day. Please note that the beads are sacred and therefore should never touch the ground or be put in an unclean place. To keep your beads clean, it is best to carry them in a special bead bag, also available from any of the temples.

Aside from chanting *japa,* you can also sing the Lord's holy names in *kīrtana.* Although you can sing *kīrtana* on your own, it is generally performed with others. A melodious *kīrtana* with family or friends is sure to enliven everyone. ISKCON devotees use traditional melodies and instruments, especially in the temple, but you can chant to any melody and use any musical instruments to accompany your chanting. As Lord Caitanya said, "There are no hard and fast rules for chanting Hare Kṛṣṇa." One thing you might want to do, however, is to obtain some *kīrtana* and *japa* audiotapes and hear the various styles of chanting.

Setting Up Your Altar

You will probably find that *japa* and *kīrtana* are more effective when done before an altar. Lord Kṛṣṇa and His pure devotees are so kind that they allow us to worship them even through their pictures. It's something like mailing a letter: You can't mail a letter by placing it in just any box; you must use the postbox authorised by the government. Similarly, we cannot concoct an image of God and worship that, but we may worship the authorised picture of God, and Kṛṣṇa accepts our worship through that picture.

Setting up an altar at home means receiving the Lord and His pure devotees as your most honoured guests. Where should you set up the altar? Well, how would you seat a guest? An ideal place would be clean, well lit, and free from draughts and household disturbances. Your guest, of course, would need a comfortable chair, but for the picture of

Kṛṣṇa's form a wall shelf, a mantel-piece, a corner table, or the top shelf of a bookcase will do. You wouldn't seat a guest in your home and then ignore him; you'd provide a place for yourself to sit, too, where you could comfortably face him and enjoy his company, so don't make your altar inaccessible.

What do you need to set up your altar? Here are the essentials:

1. A picture of Śrīla Prabhupāda.
2. A picture of Lord Caitanya and His associates.
3. A picture of Rādhā and Kṛṣṇa.

In addition, you may want an altar cloth, water cups (one for each picture), candles with holders, a special plate for offering food, a small bell, incense, an incense holder, and fresh flowers, which you may offer in vases or simply place before each picture. If you're interested in more elaborate Deity worship, ask any of the ISKCON devotees or write to the Bhaktivedanta Book Trust.

The first person we worship on the altar is the spiritual master. The spiritual master is not God. Only God is God. But because the spiritual master is His dearmost servant, God has empowered him to be His representative and therefore he deserves the same respect as that given to God. The spiritual master links the disciple with God and teaches him the process of *bhakti-yoga.* He is God's ambassador to the material world. When the Queen sends an ambassador to a foreign country, the ambassador receives the same respect as that accorded the Queen, and the ambassador's words are as authoritative as the Queen's. Similarly, we should respect the spiritual master as we would God, and revere his words as we would God's.

There are two main kinds of *guru*: the instructing *guru* and the initiating *guru.* Everyone who takes up the process of *bhakti-yoga* as a result of coming in contact with ISKCON owes an immense debt of gratitude to Śrīla Prabhupāda. Before Śrīla Prabhupāda left India in 1965 to spread Kṛṣṇa consciousness abroad, almost no one outside India knew anything about the practice of pure devotional service to Lord Kṛṣṇa. Therefore, everyone who has learned of the process through his books, his *Back to Godhead* magazine, his tapes, or contact with his followers should offer respect to Śrīla Prabhupāda. As the founder and spiritual guide of the International Society for Krishna Consciousness, he is the prime instructing *guru* of all of us.

Devotees should first of all develop this spiritual understanding and their relationship with Śrīla Prabhupāda. However, the Vedic literature encourages us to become connected to the current link of the chain of spiritual masters. Following Śrīla Prabhupāda's departure, this means accepting initiation from one of Śrīla Prabhupāda's senior followers who are acknowledged as spiritual masters within the movement.

The second picture on your altar should be of the *pañca-tattva,* Lord Caitanya and His four leading associates. Lord Caitanya is the incarnation of God for this age. He is Kṛṣṇa Himself, descended in the form of His own devotee to teach us how to surrender to Him, specifically by chanting His holy names and performing other activities of *bhakti-yoga.* Lord Caitanya is the most merciful incarnation, for He makes it easy for anyone to attain love of God through the chanting of the Hare Kṛṣṇa *mantra.*

And of course, your altar should have a picture of the Supreme Personality of Godhead, Lord Śrī Kṛṣṇa, with His eternal consort, Śrīmatī Rādhārāṇī. Śrīmatī Rādhārāṇī is Kṛṣṇa's spiritual potency. She is devotional service personified, and devotees always take shelter of Her to learn how to serve Kṛṣṇa.

You can arrange the pictures in a triangle, with the picture of Śrīla Prabhupāda on the left, the picture of Lord Caitanya and His associates on the right and the picture of Rādhā and Kṛṣṇa, which, if possible, should be slightly larger than the others, on a small raised platform behind and in the centre. Or you can hang the picture of Rādhā and Kṛṣṇa on the wall above.

When you establish an altar, you are inviting Kṛṣṇa and His pure devotees to reside as the most important guests in your home. Carefully clean the altar each morning. Cleanliness is essential in the worship of Kṛṣṇa. You would not neglect to clean the room of an important guest. If you have water cups, rinse them out and fill them with fresh water daily. Then place them conveniently close to the pictures. You should remove flowers in vases as soon as they're slightly wilted, or daily if you've offered them at the base of the pictures. You should offer fresh incense at least once a day, and, if possible, light candles and place them near the pictures while you're chanting before the altar.

Please try the things we've suggested so far. It's very simple really: If you try to love God, you'll gradually realize how much He loves you. That's the essence of *bhakti-yoga.*

Prasādam: How to Eat Spiritually

By His omnipotent transcendental energies, Kṛṣṇa can actually convert matter into spirit. If we place an iron rod in a fire, soon the rod becomes red hot and acts just like fire. In the same way, food prepared for and offered to Kṛṣṇa with love and devotion becomes completely spiritualized. Such food is called Kṛṣṇa *prasādam,* which means "the mercy of Lord Kṛṣṇa".

Eating *prasādam* is a fundamental practice of *bhakti-yoga.* In other forms of *yoga* one must artificially repress the senses, but the *bhakti-yogī* can engage his or her senses in a variety of pleasing spiritual activities, such as tasting delicious food offered to Lord Kṛṣṇa. In this way the senses gradually become spiritualised and bring the devotee more and more transcendental pleasure by being engaged in devotional service. Such spiritual pleasure far surpasses any kind of material experience.

Lord Caitanya said of *prasādam,* "Everyone has tasted these foods before. However, now that they have been prepared for Kṛṣṇa and offered to Him with devotion, these foods have acquired extraordinary tastes and uncommon fragrances. Just taste them and see the difference in experience! Apart from the taste, even the fragrance pleases the mind and makes one forget any other aroma. Therefore, it should be understood that the spiritual nectar of Kṛṣṇa's lips must have touched these ordinary foods and imparted to them all their transcendental qualities."

Eating only food offered to Kṛṣṇa is the perfection of vegetarianism. Refraining from animal flesh out of compassion for innocent creatures is certainly a praiseworthy sentiment, but when we go beyond vegetarianism to a diet of *prasādam,* our eating becomes helpful in achieving the goal of human life — reawakening the soul's original relationship with God. In the *Bhagavad-gītā* Lord Kṛṣṇa says that unless one eats only food that has been offered to Him in sacrifice, one will suffer the reactions of *karma.*

How to Prepare and Offer Prasādam

As you walk down the supermarket aisles selecting the foods you will offer to Kṛṣṇa, you need to know what is offerable and what is not. In the *Bhagavad-gītā,* Lord Kṛṣṇa states, "If one offers Me with love and devotion a leaf, a flower, a fruit, or water, I will accept it." Elsewhere, it is explained that we can offer Kṛṣṇa foods prepared from milk products, vegetables, fruits, nuts, and grains. (Write to the

Bhaktivedanta Book Trust for one of the many Hare Kṛṣṇa cookbooks.) Meat, fish and eggs are not offerable. A few vegetarian items are also forbidden — garlic and onions, for example, because they tend to agitate the mind, making meditation more difficult. (Hing, asafoetida, is a tasty substitute for them in cooking and is available at most Indian grocers.) Nor can you offer Kṛṣṇa coffee or tea that contain caffeine. If you like these beverages, purchase caffeine-free coffee and herbal teas.

While shopping, be aware that you may find meat, fish, and egg products mixed with other foods; so be sure to read labels carefully. For instance, some brands of yoghurt and sour cream contain gelatin, a substance made from the horns, hooves, and bones of slaughtered animals. Most hard cheese contains rennet, an enzyme extracted from the stomach tissue of slaughtered calves. Look for such cheese labelled as being suitable for vegetarians.

Try to avoid foods cooked by nondevotees. According to the subtle laws of nature the consciousness of the cook affects the food. The principle is the same as that at work in a painting: a painting is not simply a collection of brush strokes on a canvas but an expression of the artist's state of mind, which affects the viewer. So if you eat food cooked by nondevotees such as processed foods etc., then you are likely to absorb a dose of materialism and *karma.* As far as possible in your own cooking use only fresh, natural ingredients.

In preparing food, cleanliness is the most important principle. Nothing impure should be offered to God; so keep your kitchen very clean. Always wash your hands thoroughly before entering the kitchen. While preparing food, do not taste it, for you are cooking the meal not for yourself but for the pleasure of Kṛṣṇa. Arrange portions of the food on dinnerware kept especially for this purpose; no one but the Lord should eat from those dishes. The easiest way to offer food is simply to pray, "My dear Lord Kṛṣṇa, please accept this food," and to chant each of the following prayers three times while ringing a bell.

1. Prayer to Śrīla Prabhupāda:

nama oṁ viṣṇu-pādāya kṛṣṇa-preṣṭhāya bhū-tale
śrīmate bhaktivedānta-svāmin iti nāmine

namas te sārasvate deve gaura-vāṇī-pracāriṇe
nirviśeṣa-śūnyavādi-pāścātya-deśa-tāriṇe

"I offer my respectful obeisances unto His Divine Grace A.C. Bhaktivedanta Swami Prabhupāda, who is very dear to Lord Kṛṣṇa, having taken shelter at His lotus feet. Our respectful obeisances are unto you, O spiritual master, servant of Bhaktisiddhānta Sarasvatī Gosvāmī. You are kindly preaching the message of Lord Caitanyadeva and delivering the Western countries, which are filled with impersonalism and voidism."

2. Prayer to Lord Caitanya:

namo mahā-vadānyāya kṛṣṇa-prema-pradāya te
kṛṣṇāya kṛṣṇa-caitanya-nāmne gaura-tviṣe namaḥ

"O most munificent incarnation! You are Kṛṣṇa Himself appearing as Śrī Kṛṣṇa Caitanya Mahāprabhu. You have assumed the golden colour of Śrīmatī Rādhārāṇī, and You are widely distributing pure love of Kṛṣṇa. We offer our respectful obeisances unto You."

3. Prayer to Lord Kṛṣṇa:

namo brahmaṇya-devāya go-brāhmaṇa-hitāya ca
jagad-dhitāya kṛṣṇāya govindāya namo namaḥ

"I offer my respectful obeisances unto Lord Kṛṣṇa, who is the worshipable Deity for all *brāhmaṇas*, the well-wisher of the cows and the *brāhmaṇas*, and the benefactor of the whole world. I offer my repeated obeisances to the Personality of Godhead, known as Kṛṣṇa and Govinda."

Remember that the real purpose of preparing and offering food to the Lord is to show your devotion and gratitude to Him. Kṛṣṇa accepts your devotion, not the physical offering itself. God is complete in Himself — He doesn't need anything — but out of His immense kindness He allows us to offer food to Him so that we can develop our love for Him.

After offering the food to the Lord, wait at least five minutes for Him to partake of the preparations. Then you should transfer the food from the special dinnerware and wash the dishes and utensils you used for the offering. Now you, your family and any guests may eat the *prasādam*. While you eat, try to appreciate the spiritual value of the food. Remember that because Kṛṣṇa has accepted it, it is nondifferent from Him, and therefore by eating it you will become purified.

Everything you offer on your altar becomes *prasādam*, the mercy of the Lord. The flowers, the incense, the water, the food having been offered for the Lord's pleasure become spiritualised. The Lord enters into the offerings, and thus the remnants are nondifferent from Him. So you should not only deeply respect the things you've offered, but you should distribute them to others as well. Distribution of *prasādam* is an essential expression of your devotion to Kṛṣṇa.

Everyday Life: The Four Regulative Principles

Anyone serious about progressing in Kṛṣṇa consciousness must try to avoid the following four sinful activities:

1. **Eating meat, fish, or eggs.** These foods are saturated with the modes of passion and ignorance, and therefore cannot be offered to the Lord. A person who eats these foods participates in a conspiracy of violence against helpless animals and thus curtails his spiritual progress.

2. **Gambling.** Gambling invariably puts one into anxiety and fuels greed, envy, and anger.

3. **The use of intoxicants.** Drugs, alcohol, and tobacco, as well as any drinks or foods containing caffeine, cloud the mind, overstimulate the senses, and make it impossible to understand or follow the principles of *bhakti-yoga.*

4. **Illicit sex.** This is sex outside of marriage or sex in marriage for any purpose other than procreation. Sex for pleasure compels one to identify with the body and prevents from understanding Kṛṣṇa consciousness. The scriptures teach that sex attraction is the most powerful force binding us to the illusions of the material world. Anyone serious about advancing in Kṛṣṇa consciousness should therefore abstain from or regulate sexual activity according to the scriptures. In *Bhagavad-gītā* Kṛṣṇa says that sexual union for conceiving a child to be raised in God consciousness is an act of devotion to Him.

Engagement in Practical Devotional Service

We all must work to earn our livelihood and to maintain home, family, and so on. However, if we try to take the fruits of our labour for ourselves and dependents, we must also accept the karmic reactions incurred because of our work. Kṛṣṇa says in the *Bhagavad-gītā* (3.9), "Work done as a sacrifice for Viṣṇu (Kṛṣṇa) has to be performed. Otherwise work binds one to the material world."

However, it is not necessary to change our occupation, we need to change our attitude. If we are striving for Kṛṣṇa consciousness, if our home has become a temple, and if we share spiritual life with our family members, then what we earn may legitimately be spent for the maintenance of our domestic affairs and the balance engaged in promoting our and others' spiritual lives. Thus, whatever we do we can see it as being part of our devotional service to Kṛṣṇa.

Further, we may also have the opportunity to use our skills and talents directly for Kṛṣṇa. If you're a writer, write for Kṛṣṇa; if you're an artist, create for Kṛṣṇa; if you're a secretary, type for Kṛṣṇa. You may also help a local temple in your spare time, and you could sacrifice some of the fruits of your work by contributing a portion of your earnings to help maintain the temple and propagate Kṛṣṇa consciousness. Some devotees buy Hare Kṛṣṇa literature and distribute it to their friends and associates, or they engage in a variety of services at the temple. There is also a wide network of devotees who gather in each other's homes for chanting, worship, and study. Write to your local temple or the Society's secretary to learn of any such programmes near you.

Additional Devotional Principles

There are many more devotional practices that can help you become Kṛṣṇa conscious. Here are two vital ones:

Studying Hare Kṛṣṇa literature. Śrīla Prabhupāda, the founder-*ācārya* of ISKCON, dedicated much of his time to writing and translating books such as the *Śrīmad-Bhāgavatam*. Hearing the words — or reading the writings — of a realised spiritual master is an essential spiritual practice. So try to set aside some time every day to read Śrīla Prabhupāda's books. You can get a free catalogue of available books and tapes from the Bhaktivedanta Book Trust.

Associating with devotees. Śrīla Prabhupāda established the Hare Kṛṣṇa movement to give people in general the chance to associate with devotees of the Lord. This is the best way to gain faith in the process of Kṛṣṇa consciousness and become enthusiastic in devotional service. Conversely, maintaining intimate connections with nondevotees slows one's spiritual progress. So try to visit the Hare Kṛṣṇa centre nearest you as often as possible.

In Closing

The beauty of Kṛṣṇa consciousness is that you can take as much as you're ready for. Kṛṣṇa Himself promises in the *Bhagavad-gītā* (2.40), "There is no loss or diminution in this endeavour, and even a little advancement on this path protects one from the most fearful type of danger." So bring Kṛṣṇa into your daily life, and we guarantee you'll feel the benefit.

Hare Kṛṣṇa!

STAY IN TOUCH

Now that you've read this book, you may like to further your interest by joining thousands of others as a member of ISKCON.

The International Society for Krishna Consciousness was founded in 1966 by the author of this book, Srila Prabhupada. The Society is dedicated to providing knowledge of Krishna and the science of Krishna consciousness as a means of achieving the highest personal happiness and spiritual fellowship among all living beings. We invite you to join us.

What Does Membership of ISKCON Mean for Me?

For an annual donation of £21 you'll receive a membership package that will keep you fully informed and involved. Here's what you receive (£25 for non UK addresses):

• BACK TO GODHEAD

The Magazine of the Hare Krishna Movement

Each issue of *Back to Godhead* has colorful photos and informative articles on topics such as:

- techniques of *mantra* meditation
- how the spiritual knowledge of the *Vedas* can bring peace, satisfaction, and success in your life
- recipes for a *karma*-free diet
- news of Hare Krishna devotees and devotional projects worldwide
- clear explanations of Vedic science and cosmology
- Krishna conscious perspectives on current affairs... and much more

• THE NAMA HATTA

ISKCON UK's newsletter covering happenings in both UK and Ireland. Articles, letters and lots of news and items of interest.

• VALUABLE DISCOUNTS

All registered members will be sent a valuable 10% Membership Discount Card to use on purchases of books, audio and video tapes, posters, incense, and all other items from UK Hare Krishna shops and the mail order department.

• VAISHNAVA CALENDAR

A beautifully illustrated 12 page wall calendar featuring some of the best of The Bhaktivedanta Book Trust paintings. It will remind you of all the important festivals and celebrations of the Krishna devotee year.

Become a member today and experience the higher taste of *bhakti-yoga.*

Application for Membership

(you can write these details out on a separate piece of paper if you wish)

I wish to be included as a member of ISKCON UK and I have enclosed payment of £21 accordingly for the next years membership. Please send my magazines to:

Surname Mr/Mrs/Ms________________________________

Forenames____

Address____

____

Postcode____________________County________________

Please make all payments out to ISKCON:

Signed____________________ Date____________________

POP

Please Return this application to:
Membership Service Dept., ISKCON,
2 St. James Rd., Watford, WDI 8EA

BHAGAVAD-GITA AS IT IS

The world's most popular edition of a timeless classic.

Throughout the ages, the world's greatest minds have turned to the *Bhagavad-gita* for answers to life's perennial questions. Renowned as the jewel of India's spiritual wisdom, the *Gita* summarizes the profound Vedic knowledge concerning man's essential nature, his environment, and ultimately his relationship with God. With more than fifty million copies sold in twenty languages, *Bhagavad-gita As It Is,* by His Divine Grace A.C. Bhaktivedanta Swami Prabhupada, is the most widely read edition of the *Gita* in the world. It includes the original Sanskrit text, phonetic transliterations, word-for-word meanings, translation, elaborate commentary, and many full-colour illustrations.

	Pocket	Vinyl	Hard	Deluxe
UK	**£3.00**	**£5.25**	**£7.95**	**£13.95**
US	$3.90	$8.50	$10.30	$18.00
AUS		$11.00	$14.00	$28.00

EASY JOURNEY TO OTHER PLANETS

One of Srila Prabhupada's earliest books, *Easy Journey* describes how *bhakti-yoga* enables us to transfer ourselves from the material to the spiritual world.

Softbound, 96 pages

UK: £1.00; US: $1.00; AUS: $2.00

BEYOND BIRTH AND DEATH

What is the self? Can it exist apart from the physical body? If so, what happens to the self at the time of death? What about reincarnation? Liberation? *Beyond Birth and Death* answers these intriguing questions, and more.

Softbound, 96 pages

UK: £1.00; US: $1.00; AUS: $2.00

THE HIGHER TASTE

A Guide to Gourmet Vegetarian Cooking and a Karma-Free Diet

Illustrated profusely with black-and-white drawings and eight full-colour plates, this popular volume contains over 60 tried and tested international recipes, together with the why's and how's of the Krishna conscious vegetarian life-style.

Softbound, 176 pages

UK: £1.00; US: $1.99; AUS: $2.00

RAJA-VIDYA: THE KING OF KNOWLEDGE

In this book we learn why knowledge of Krishna is absolute and frees the soul from material bondage.

Softbound, 128 pages

UK: £1.00; US: $1.00; AUS: $2.00

THE PERFECTION OF YOGA

A lucid explanation of the psychology, techniques, and purposes of *yoga;* a summary and comparison of the different *yoga* systems; and an introduction to meditation.

Softbound, 96 pages

UK: £1.00; US: $1.00; AUS: $2.00

MESSAGE OF GODHEAD

An excerpt: "The influences of various people, places, and terms have led us to designate ourselves as Hindus, Muslims, Christians, Buddhists, Socialists, Bolsheviks, and so forth. But when we attain transcendental knowledge and are established in *sanatana-dharma,* the actual, eternal religion of the living entity, the spirit soul, then and then only can we attain real, undeniable peace, prosperity, and happiness in this world."

Softbound, 68 pages

UK: £1.00; US: $1.00; AUS: $2.00

STAY IN TOUCH...

❐ Please send me a free information pack, including the small booklet *Krishna the Reservoir of Pleasure* and a catalogue of available books.

- ❐ Bhagavad-gita As It Is ❐ Pocket ❐ Vinyl ❐ Hard ❐ Deluxe
- ❐ Great Vegetarian Dishes
- ❐ The Hare Krishna Book of Vegetarian Cooking
- ❐ The Higher Taste
- ❐ Raja-Vidya: The King of Knowledge
- ❐ Easy Journey to Other Planets
- ❐ Beyond Birth and Death
- ❐ The Perfection of Yoga
- ❐ Message of Godhead

Please send me the above books. I enclose $/£_______ to cover the cost and understand that the prices given include postage and packaging. (All prices offered here are greatly reduced from our normal retail charges!)

Name____
PLEASE PRINT

Address____

____________________________ Postcode_______________

POP

Post this form with payment to:

In Europe: The Bhaktivedanta Book Trust, P.O. Box 324, Borehamwood, Herts, WD6 1NB, U.K.

In North America: The Bhaktivedanta Book Trust, 3764 Watseka Ave., Los Angeles, CA 90034, U.S.A.

In Australasia: The Bhaktivedanta Book Trust, P.O. Box 262, Botany, N.S.W. 2019, Australia

BOOKS by His Divine Grace A. C. Bhaktivedanta Swami Prabhupāda

Bhagavad-gītā As It Is
Śrīmad-Bhāgavatam, cantos 1-10 (12 vols.)
Śrī Caitanya-caritāmṛta (17 vols.)
Teachings of Lord Caitanya
The Nectar of Devotion
The Nectar of Instruction
Śrī Īśopaniṣad
Easy Journey to Other Planets
Kṛṣṇa Consciousness: The Topmost Yoga System
Kṛṣṇa, The Supreme Personality of Godhead
Perfect Questions, Perfect Answers
Teachings of Lord Kapila, the Son of Devahūti
Transcendental Teachings of Prahlāda Mahārāja
Teachings of Queen Kuntī
Kṛṣṇa, the Reservoir of Pleasure
The Science of Self-Realization
The Path of Perfection
Search for Liberation
The Journey of Self-Discovery
A Second Chance
Laws of Nature
Message of Godhead
Civilization and Transcendence
Life Comes From Life
The Perfection of Yoga
Beyond Birth and Death
On the Way to Kṛṣṇa
Rāja-vidyā: The King of Knowledge
Elevation to Kṛṣṇa Consciousness
Kṛṣṇa Consciousness: The Matchless Gift
Back to Godhead magazine (founder)

available from

The Bhaktivedanta Book Trust
P.O. Box 324, Borehamwood
Herts. WD6 1NB, England
Telephone: 081-905 1244

The Bhaktivedanta Book Trust
3764 Watseka Avenue
Los Angeles, California 90034
USA

The Bhaktivedanta Book Trust
P.O. Box 262
Botany, N.S.W. 2019
Australia